OLD NEWGATE GATEWAY, 1750
The Windmill was for ventilation
(from old print in British Museum)

PUNISHMENTS OF FORMER DAYS
Ernest W Pettifer

This reprint
Published in 1992 by
WATERSIDE PRESS
Domum Road
Winchester
SO23 9NN

First edition published by the author in 1939
Second edition published by the author in 1947

Book orders for reprint:
WATERSIDE PRESS
Freepost
Winchester
Hants
SO23 9BR

0962 855567

ISBN Paperback 1 872870 05 8

Printing and binding Antony Rowe Ltd, Chippenham, Wiltshire

PUNISHMENTS OF FORMER DAYS

by
ERNEST W. PETTIFER

Clerk to the West Riding Justices, Doncaster

January 21st, 1664.

"Up, and after sending my wife to my Aunt Wright's to get a place to see Turner hanged, I to the 'Change; and seeing people flock to the City, I enquired, and found that Turner was not yet hanged. And so I went among them to Leadenhall Street, at the end of Lyme Street, near where the robbery was done; and to St. Mary Axe, where he lived. And there I got for a shilling to stand upon the wheel of a cart, in great pain, above an hour before the execution was done; he delaying the time by long discourses and prayers one after another, in hopes of a reprieve; but none come, and at last was flung off the ladder in his cloak. A comely-looked man he was, and kept his countenance to the end; I was sorry to see him. It was believed there were at least 12 or 14,000 people in the street."

(The Diary of Samuel Pepys, Esq., F.R.S.)

WATERSIDE PRESS
WINCHESTER

CONTENTS

LIST OF ILLUSTRATIONS

PRISON CHAMBER IN THE GATEWAY OF HOOTON
PAGNELL HALL, NEAR DONCASTER

Foreword to First Edition

This book is not intended to be, in any sense, a history of punishments. There is already in existence a clear and exhaustive account of many forms of punishment in the volume, first published in 1881, by the late Mr. William Andrews, of Hull, entitled "Punishments in the Olden Times." A larger volume by the same author appeared in 1890, under the title "Old Time Punishments." How much thought and research Mr. Andrews gave to this book can be gathered from his own statement that he consulted several hundred works, drew facts from ancient prints and manuscripts, and ransacked files of daily and weekly newspapers for his facts and illustrations.

Under yet another title, "Bygone Punishments," a third edition of his book appeared in 1931, with a foreword by his son, Mr. W. L. Andrews, the editor of the "Leeds Mercury," so that it is evident that no further history of the subject is yet necessary.

The notes for this book had been largely prepared in the form of articles in the "West Riding Police Journal," when I was introduced to Mr. Andrews' book by a friend, and it was the discovery of how much could be written upon this most interesting phase of history that ultimately led me to a decision to expand my own brief notes into a small book which could be read as an introduction to the story told so ably and interestingly by Mr. Andrews.

Here, then, is my apology for undertaking a task which has given me much pleasure, and which has taught me much concerning the enforcement and the methods of punishments in former days. It has also given me new light upon the brutalities and deliberate cruelties of those days, and has brought a greater realisation of the debt we owe, as a great country to the labours and faith of the men and women who toiled on, in the dark days, to win for the wrong-doer a wise and tolerant system of justice, and more merciful and reasonable methods of punishment.

A certain section of those who claim to be reformers of our penal methods to-day, could learn much from the Christian reasonableness, the deep sincerity, and the self-sacrifice of those who laboured, in face of great difficulties, but with an unconquerable hope, in the evil days, now long past. Minor improvements may still be necessary, for instance, in our prison system, but, in the present day, there is little ground for the unreasonable criticisms of the few agitators who appear to ignore the fact that prisons are for the criminals, and not for the afflicted and the wronged.

William Andrews, in the words of his son, "was a social reformer, with an ardent faith in the perfectibility of human nature." Such a faith should live in us all, even though it be sometimes rudely shaken by the stories told in the criminal courts of the country. I trust that these sketches may help to maintain that faith, as well as to bring to our consideration of the penal methods of to-day some little knowledge of the evil methods of less humane times.

While I freely, and gladly, acknowledge my indebtedness to Mr. Andrews' book, I would say that the bulk of the information which I have compiled has come from sources untouched by his book. There is a mass of information scattered through many books which is valuable and interesting. It is not necessary always to go to books like "Bygone Punishments" for facts and illustrations upon such a subject.

Our history books—Hume, Innes, and J. R. Green, for instance—are full of instructive and suggestive incidents from our penal history. Among the novelists and other writers, Scott, Dickens, Sir Walter Besant, Rafael Sabatini, Sir A. Conan Doyle, H. V. Morton and many others furnish vivid illustrations of the application of former methods of trial and punishment, and give a reliable historical background to such matters as trial by combat, prison life, benefit of clergy, public hangings, sanctuary, the pillory, etc.

There are some writers and speakers of to-day who speak as hysterically of our present penal system as they, probably, would have done had they lived a hundred and fifty years ago, in the days of old-time punishments, but it is necessary to keep a sense of proportion, and to avoid false sentiment.

It is little more than a century ago since the criminal had proved conclusively that the existing police system could not cope with him. In the gloomy days of the eighteenth century, to go back no further into history, the fear of the criminal overshadowed the people, and our national life. Few evil-doers were captured; hundreds escaped; and the fear of the nation was expressed by their acquiescence in the merciless and cruel retaliation meted out to the captured by the Judges and Justices, in their efforts to stem the growing tide

The reorganisation of the police forces, which was carried out in the first half of the nineteenth century, proved at last the soundness of the theory held by far-seeing magistrates such as Sir Henry and Sir John Fielding in the dark days of the eighteenth century, that an organised and efficient police force must always prove more than a match for the individual criminal.

A study of the methods employed by a nation against its wrong-doers is not a cheerful one at any time, but when that nation is fear-ridden and resorts to intolerance, cruelty and ruthlessness, the record becomes a depressing one indeed. We have long ago learnt the lesson that cruelty and justice cannot go hand in hand, and have abandoned angry and revengeful punishments because they create more ills than they can cure. To-day, whatever a few extremists may claim, cruelty has no place in the English penal system, and the pillory and the rack, the stocks and the branding iron, found now only in our museums, are but reminders of evil days long passed away.

These revolting instruments of punishment, familiar enough to our great-grandfathers, are now almost forgotten, but they are faithful witnesses to a black page—many pages—in English history and as such, they still have a historic interest. They explain the determination of those administering justice; of those in control of the police forces of to-day; and of the great majority of thinking people that methods of dealing with the law-breaker shall be firmly based upon justice, sympathy and a continued attempt to appreciate the mind and the temptations of the criminal.

Unfortunately, the public of to-day, as in past centuries, have little real knowledge of the police and penal system of the day, and they are easily swayed and misled by the so-called reformers, who include not only those sentimental people to whom the infliction of pain in any form is repellant, but those who would like to see all punishment swept away as mere revenge and retaliation.

It is freely claimed by these critics that crime is merely a disease, or a temporary aberration of the criminal. It is neither, in the vast majority of crimes. It is an act done by the deliberate choice of the criminal. A well-known Judge recently said, "My experience in trying and sentencing prisoners at the Assizes and the Old Bailey has satisfied me that crime is not a disease, and that what I call the criminal classes mainly consist of ordinary citizens who have fallen into and given way to temptation." This, in a few words, is the experience of all who have had long experience of the administration of courts of justice. To attempt the reform of the criminal is commendable, but, in the interests of the great body of the people, he must also he deterred from further crime, or the life of the people will become as perilous as it was in the days when the criminal had mastered the forces for law and order.

Too little attention is given to-day to the grievous wrongs suffered by countless people owing to the evil acts of the criminal—the physical injuries sometimes leaving permanent ill-effects; the financial loss; the cruelties to women and children; the trail of misery, pain and loss left by even one year's crimes. A man had a quarrel with another man in a public-house. Outside, he struck an innocent passer-by, mistaking him for his opponent, and fractured his skull. When the injured man recovered consciousness he was mentally deranged, and spent four years in an asylum before he partially recovered to return to his wife and four children. During those four years the wife and family lived on poor relief. The violent brute who caused all this suffering received eighteen months' hard labour. Much thought is given to-day, officially and unofficially, to make the lot of such an offender in prison as comfortable as possible, whilst a wife and four children struggle along for four years (for over two and a half years after the man who caused their suffering had been released from prison) on a State pittance carefully calculated just to keep them above the starvation line. If the advocates of "prison reform" could be persuaded to divert their energies and resources to alleviating some of the misery caused by the criminal, they could do a far more effective work for the nation .

The question as to whether corporal punishment is to continue will, in all probability, have been settled before these words appear in print. It has been brought before Parliament, at last, after a noisy but effective campaign, carried out, again, by the few who have made up their minds that the criminal must not suffer physical pain, whatever his victim may have suffered from his wrong-doing. His Majesty's Judges and Justices have not been consulted as to their views; neither have the police forces of the country. On behalf of the general public it is stated, veraciously, that they are opposed to corporal punishment. There are, of course, two distinct matters involved in this punishment—the whipping of children, and the flogging of violent rogues.

There was an interesting comment upon the whipping of boys recently, by a mother of one of a gang of boys all ordered to be birched. She was very angry when the sentence was passed, but, when invited by the police to see the punishment carried out, as she had a right to do, she consented. Her comment made at the time, was "Why, it's nowt; I've done worse to him many a time myself"!

While the number of floggings has gone down for many years past, juvenile crime has gone up by great strides, thousands more crimes being committed each year. No further proof of this statement is needed than the Criminal Statistics published annually by the Home Office. The only reform necessary in this case is the substitution of the cane for the birch, and, possibly, the power to Justices to suspend the execution of the punishment for a given period, with a view to seeing whether the threat of a caning acts as a deterrent to further wrong-doing.

The flogging of the violent criminal is a different matter. There are many criminals, naturally brutal and unprincipled men, who are only deterred from violent robberies by the fear of consequences. The Criminal Statistics, again, prove that, while floggings have increased, such offences have become far fewer. It is idle to argue that some of these men commit further offences—so do men sentenced to penal servitude or imprisonment. The only valid criticism is that flogging is now confined to robbery with violence, and not permitted in cases of offences against women, where fear or violence are employed. The "black list" cases at Assize after Assize are sufficient proof of the dreadful wrongs inflicted by callous, selfish men upon women and girls, and, when physical and mental pain of this type is inflicted upon the defenceless, pain is the appropriate punishment for the brutal perpetrators of such wrongs.

I must acknowledge the willing help and the courtesy of everyone who has contributed to the matter, and the illustrations, in this book. I can recall no single instance of a refusal of any request; on the other hand there are scores of kindly people who have given me cause to remember with pleasure and appreciation their contributions and assistance. I wish I could name them all. Mr. J. R. Witty, B.A., of Beverley, a well-known and gifted authority on Beverley Minster, and its sanctuary customs, has given me generous help in compiling the chapters on "Sanctuary" and "A Yorkshire Sanctuary." Mr. W. Eden Hooper, the author of "The History of Newgate and the Old Bailey," and his publishers (the Underwood Press, Ltd.) willingly gave me a free hand to quote from that valuable work, and to use the illustrations. Messrs. Philip Allen & Co., Ltd. (publishers of "Bygone

Punishments"), Major F. R. Hedges (of Wallingford Castle, Berks.), Madame Tussaud's, Ltd., the British Museum, Messrs. Ramsden (photographic artists, of Leicester) and others have willingly assisted me with regard to photographs. The West Riding Police have given me valuable assistance, in the collection of matter, and the preparation of photographs and blocks.

I would mention Mr. J. Cooper (Junior), Clerk to the Justices at Beverley, and Mr. A. J. Chislett, Chief Clerk at Westminster Police Court, for their friendly and practical interest in several of my subjects, and the Berkshire, Norfolk Warwick and other County Police forces, who have willingly gone to considerable trouble for me on various points which arose from time to time.

ERNEST W. PETTIFER

Burghclere,
   Bessacarr,
      Doncaster
April, 1939

Foreword to Second Edition

The first edition of this book was soon sold, but, owing to the war conditions, it was impossible to reprint it earlier. Since the book was written I have received many items of interest from kindly correspondents, and I hoped to include these in a second edition, but the difficult conditions with regard to printing and paper compel me to re-issue the book in its original form, with the exception of a few additional notes.

I would acknowledge, with sincere thanks, the kindness of my correspondents and would assure them that I hope, in a later edition, to introduce the additional facts and incidents which have come to hand.

ERNEST W. PETTIFER

Burghclere,
   Bessacarr,
      Doncaster.
March, 1947

Ernest Pettifer - A Note

I was introduced to Ernest Pettifer's book *Punishments of Former Days* by my predecessor Tony Hudson in 1976. It was one of three dusty volumes handed to me on his retirement, as if for safe-keeping. The others were *The Court Is Sitting* (1940) and *The Court Resumes* (1945). All three books are signed by the author and in one of them was a handwritten note, on the back of an old compliments slip, in which Ernest Pettifer recalls his early days '. . . in the lovely countryside of South Berkshire and North Hampshire'.

The books proved fascinating, perhaps because they encapsulated a style and an era long gone. There is also the unusual feature that Ernest Pettifer published his books privately, having them printed by Clegg and Son Ltd. of Bradford and distributing them through a local bookseller and by direct mail from the West Riding Court House at Doncaster. Some years later I resolved to try and get *Punishments of Former Days* into print again, for the benefit of people who might have a similar interest. This was easier said than done.

Ernest Pettifer died in 1962. By then he had become a frequent contributor to *Justice of the Peace*, and to other journals and newspapers. He wrote, primarily, on aspects of legal history, but also had an eye for the issues of the day. His first article was published in 1938. His final article was still in the typewriter, unfinished, when he died. It was published posthumously. Ernest Pettifer was clerk to the justices at Doncaster for 45 years. He served on the council of the Justices' Clerks' Society and was president of that Society in 1947-8. He was an 'unadmitted man', himself the son of a clerk to the justices. In an article he recalls starting work in his father's office in Newbury at the age of 14. He was awarded the honorary degree of Master of Arts by Sheffield University in 1954.

He was well respected and, it transpires, fondly remembered by everyone. In the course of my inquiries I unearthed anecdote upon anecdote concerning a 'warm, friendly man', of immense scholarship, ability, humour and diversity of interests (Not least was one recollection to the effect that EWP was no mean athlete and, in his younger days, a bare-knuckle fighter. The description 'Iron Man' was mentioned during that particular conversation!).

Nine months, many telephone calls and several false trails later (including the discovery of a—no doubt surprised—legal namesake on Humberside), a letter published in *Justice of the Peace* brought results. A son had entered the ministry, so recalled Bill Scott OBE, a former justices' clerk, and Ernest Pettifer's one time principal assistant at Doncaster. The Synod of the Church of England and Crockford's Directory led me to Bryan Pettifer (then Canon of St. Alban's Cathedral) and contact with Ernest Pettifer's wife Muriel who lives in Devon and who readily agreed to this reprint when asked.

Thanks are also due to several other people who helped to point me in the right direction, including: Ben Hartwell OBE, His Honour Judge John Henham, Len Parmenter, Barry Rose MBE, Colonel W. K. Angus OBE, TD, George Whiteside OBE, Anthony Draycott OBE and Peter Jackson.

Punishments of Former Days was first published in 1939. A review of the second edition (1947) published in *The Justices' Clerk* records:

> . . . Just before the outbreak of war in 1939, Mr Ernest W. Pettifer, the clerk to the West Riding Justices, Doncaster, published a most interesting book called *Punishments of Former Days*. The first edition was soon sold out, and, owing to war conditions, it was impossible to reprint it until recently . . . Mr. Pettifer states in his preface that the preparation of this book has given him much pleasure. There can be no doubt that a perusal of this little volume will be of much interest to the reader.

That review also mentions Ernest Pettifer's immense scholarship, the same scholarship which caused *Justice of the Peace* to comment, by way of tribute, in 1962, that Ernest Pettifer was:

> . . . probably the country's leading authority on Justices from the Tudor and Stuart periods, although from his innate sense of modesty one would never learn this from Pettifer himself.

This reprint reflects the original text, as far as is possible. The typesetting, punctuation, style and, in some instances, contemporary usages (which may sometimes seem strange by modern comparison) have been left intact, thus preserving the complete integrity of the work. All the original photographs and illustrations are reproduced. It has not been possible to exceed the original quality of these, of course, which, in a few cases was (again by modern standards) already borderline. I hope that the final result is as Ernest Pettifer would have wished—the text itself loses nothing from the passage of time. In fact, it may gain something, not least as a record of the views of someone at the centre of summary justice earlier this century. It seems quite fitting that publication should coincide with the thirtieth anniversary of Ernest Pettifer's final article.

BRYAN GIBSON
June 1992

BIRDCAGE WALK, OR DEAD MAN'S WALK, IN NEWGATE
GAOL AT TIME OF DEMOLITION

CHAPTER I.

CRIME AND PUNISHMENT IN THE EIGHTEENTH CENTURY

The penal code of the eighteenth and early nineteenth centuries was an almost unbelievably savage one.

The forest laws of the Normans are frequently quoted as the most brutal laws ever enforced against the English people, yet, in 1819, seven hundred years later, a Committee of the House of Lords was assured by a witness that, at that date, there were two hundred and twenty offences on the statute-book, punishable by death. The misery caused by the penal system, a system directed against members of a free country and not against a captive race such as the English were under the Normans, was aggravated by a multitude of other cruelties, - dreadful prison conditions, savage whippings, the stocks and pillory, the outlawing of thousands of men and women by transportation, the merciless infliction of degradation and pain upon all who were held to have offended against the law.

Death had become the cure for all but the most trivial crimes, the remedy for nearly all felonies. Offences which, to-day, would be dealt with by admonition and a small fine, or helpful periods of probation, such as damaging shrubs in public gardens; larceny of property over the value of a shilling; breaking down the head of a fishpond so that the fish might escape; cutting a hop-bind in a hop plantation; and a hundred others, were all punishable by death by hanging.

[margin note: against title / can get away with murder]

The commission of any one of these two hundred and twenty crimes placed a man or woman outside the reach of pity or of hope. Men were afraid of the criminal, so they disposed of him savagely and summarily. Yet, throughout the centuries, there had always been men who were disquieted by this attitude towards the offender. Just four hundred years ago, in the reign of Henry VIII., Sir Thomas More laid down principles which are accepted without question to-day. He pleaded for proportion between the punishment and the crime. He pointed out the folly of the cruel penalties of the day in which he lived. "Simple theft is not so great an offence as to be punished with death," he said. If a thief and a murderer were sure of the same penalty, he urged, the law was simply tempting the thief to murder his victim so that he should tell no tales. The end of all punishment he declared to be reformation. Above all, he urged that, to be remedial, punishment must be wrought out by labour and hope, so that "none is hopeless or in dispair to recover again his former state of freedom . . . so that he will ever after that live a true and honest man." Sound and unanswerable principles, accepted and applied to-day in dealing with our

[margin note: Sir Thomas More calls for equal punishment to crime]

17

offenders, yet, in the reign in which they were laid down 72,000 persons lost their lives on the scaffold, and Sir Thomas More himself, Speaker of the House of Commons, and later, Chancellor of England, lost his own head by the executioner's axe.

In the reign of Elizabeth the yearly number of executions was at least 800 and may have been considerably more; and so the slaughter went on, in reign after reign, century by century, until, coming to a time a little over a hundred and fifty years ago, the records show that, at the Lent Assizes in 1785, 242 persons were sentenced to death, 103 actually being hanged.

The files of old newspapers afford significant and tragic evidence of the severity of punishments in the eighteenth century. The man who stole was lucky if he escaped with his life. The community could not be burdened with the criminal so it killed him, thereby keeping down the prison population, and, in theory, at any rate, intimidating other wrong-doers.

The following is an extract from the "Morning Post" of January 17th, 1788:-

"Old Bailey.

A few other trials of little consequence having been finished, the Recorder, *in his usual feeling manner*, proceeded to pass sentence upon the different prisoners, when the following received sentence of death:-

James Selbin and Robert Fossett, for burglaries. Both recommended to the jury on account of their youth.

George Green and James Francis (soldiers) for robbing Mr. Evans in Hyde Park.

Thomas Collings, for highway robbery.

Robert Watson and Thomas Tuck, for horse-stealing. The former recommended to mercy by the jury.

Daniel Cunter, for returning from transportation before the term of his sentence was expired.

The five pirates under sentence of death at Newgate, will be executed this morning on a platform at Execution Dock, Wapping."

The story of the "river pirates" of this period is so interesting, and throws such a light upon the state of crime in London, that a brief explanation is necessary as to what was behind the execution of the five pirates mentioned above. The story shews how, in one part of London alone, a vicious penal system, and an inefficient police force, had, between them, led to an astounding state of lawlessness.

The pirates who met their fate at Execution Dock were probably unlucky members of that vast fraternity who, in the eighteenth century terrorised and plundered the shipping on the Thames. Sir Walter Besant has left a remarkable description of their activities in his "As we are, and as we may be."

"The people of the riverside were all, to a man, river pirates; by day and night they stole from the ships. There were often as many as a thousand vessels lying in the river : There were many hundreds of boats, barges and lighters engaged upon their cargoes. They practised their robberies in a thousand ingenious ways; they weighed the anchors and stole them; they cut adrift the lighters when they were loaded; and when they had floated down the river they pillaged what they could carry and left the rest to sink or swim; they waited till night and then rowed off to half-laden lighters and helped themselves.

Sometimes they went on board the ships as stevedores and tossed bales overboard to a confederate in the boat below; or they were coopers who carried under their aprons bags which they filled with sugar from the casks; or they took with them bladders for stealing the rum.

Some waded about in the mud at low tide to catch anything that was thrown to them from the ships. Some obtained admission to the ships as rat-catchers, and in that capacity were able to steal plunder previously concealed by their friends. Some called "scuffle-hunters" stood on the quays as porters, carrying bags under their long white aprons in which to hide whatever they could pilfer.

All this was carried on by the riverside people. They had as their accomplices the whole of the population of the quarter where they lived. The thieves were known amongst themselves by fancy names, which at once indicated the special line of each, and showed the popularity of their calling— they were bold pirates, night plunderers, light horsemen, heavy horsemen, mudlarks, game lightermen, scuffle-hunters, and gangmen. Their thefts enabled them to live on the coarse profusion of meat and drink, which they all wanted; yet they were always poor because their plunder was knocked down for so little. They saved nothing, and they were always egged on to new robberies by the men who sold them drinks, by the women who took their money from them, and by the "honest" merchants who attended the secret markets.

When they were caught it was at Execution Dock that they met their end, in full sight of their comrades and fellow thieves."

In 1792, John Harriott, a retired naval officer, was appointed a police magistrate, with special powers to deal with the river pirates, and, after two years of most exciting events, he practically put down river piracy, and reduced smuggling to a minimum. The savings to the merchants and ship-owners was estimated at half a million pounds per annum.

In the rest of London, at the same period, it was believed that there were over three thousand receivers of stolen goods, and that the property purloined each year amounted to at least £700,000. There were at least fifty fraudulent mints, and one coiner acknowledged that, in seven years, he had turned out half-crowns to the nominal value of £200,000.

A writer of 1828 asserted that thieves of the most expert kind infested every inn-yard, and awaited the coming in of the stage-coaches, mails and even wagons; the visitor intending to see London was warned that he would probably be robbed, and perhaps assaulted; that "smashers" (thieves who dealt in bad coins) might accuse the pedestrian of passing such coins, and raise the "hue and cry." He asserted that women pickpockets were numerous and expert, but that, thanks to the Robin Redbreasts (the Bow Street runners, who wore red waistcoats) highwaymen were comparatively rare. So late as 1822, he said, a party of rioters terrorised Smithfield and its neighbourhood during the night and early morning before St. Bartholomew's Fair. These ruffians paraded the streets in thousands, without let or hindrance, for the patrol and watchmen feared to interfere with so overwhelming a force, and left the rioters alone to exhaust themselves by their own fury.

These are but glimpses of the London of the early nineteenth century.

The success of Captain Harriott proved conclusively that organised police methods could achieve far more to bring within control the appalling volume of crime than had been achieved by centuries of public hangings, transportations, imprisonments and whippings; but it was many years before the people, and Parliament, took the lesson to heart.

In the meantime, the old methods were applied at Assize after Assize, Quarter Sessions after Quarter Sessions. Two more illustrations from the newspaper files for 1788:-

From the "Yorkshire Journal," October 20th, 1788.

"At the Sheffield October Quarter Sessions on this date two women were privately whipped for vagrancy, and one man was whipped in public for neglecting his family. Two men were transported for life, two more men whipped in public, one man imprisoned for one month and to be privately whipped for a common assault, and a woman imprisoned in York Castle for a year for an assault."

From the "Morning Post," March 29th, 1788.

"At Kingston Assizes yesterday, George Stock, and two others, brothers, were capitally convicted of horse stealing, and immediately received sentence of death.

One Clark, an accomplice, who turned King's evidence, contributed greatly to the conviction of Stock, and has also discovered many others of the gang, several of whom have been capitally convicted at the Assizes in the different counties."

The nineteenth century, during its opening years, offered little hope for any amelioration of the penal methods in force.

It was in 1816 that Townsend, the old Bow Street runner, gave evidence before a Royal Commission, and he said that he remembered, after one Old Bailey sitting, seeing forty persons hanging outside Newgate.

W. H. Hudson, in his intimate and moving story, "A Shepherd's Life," gives extracts from the newspapers of this period. He says, "In reading the old reports and the expressions used by the judges in their summings-up and sentences, it is impossible not to believe that the awful power they possessed, and its constant exercise, had not only produced the inevitable hardening effect, but had made them cruel in the true sense of the word. Their pleasure in passing dreadful sentences was very thinly disguised, indeed, by certain lofty conventional phrases as to the necessity of upholding the law, morality and religion; they were, indeed as familiar with the name of the Diety as any ranter in a convecticle, and the "enormity of the crime" was an expression as constantly used in the case of the theft of a loaf of bread, or of an old coat left hanging on the hedge, by some ill-clad, half-starved wretch, as in the cases of

A PUBLIC EXECUTION OUTSIDE NEWGATE GAOL

NEWGATE CHAPEL IN 1809 (Condemned criminals and coffin in the centre)

burglary, arson, rape and murder."

"It is surprising," he says, to find how very few the real crimes were in those days, despite the misery of the people; that nearly all the crimes to which men were sentenced to the gallows and to transportation for life, or for long terms, were offences which would now be sufficiently punished by a few weeks', or even a few days', imprisonment.

"Thus in April, 1825, I note that Mr. Justice Park commented on the heavy appearance of the calendar. It was not so much the number (170) of the offenders that excited his concern as it was the nature of the crimes with which they were charged. The worst crime in this case was sheep stealing.

"Again, this same Mr. Justice Park, at the Spring Assizes at Salisbury, 1827, said that though the calendar was a heavy one, he was happy to find on looking at the depositions of the principal cases, that they were not of a very serious character. Nevertheless, he passed sentence of death on 28 persons, among them being one for stealing half a crown!

"I find another case of a sentence of transportation for life on a youth of 18, named Edward Baker, for stealing a pocket handkerchief. Had he pleaded guilty it might have been worse for him.

"At the Salisbury Spring Assizes, 1830, Mr. Justice Gazalee, addressing the grand jury, said that none of the crimes appeared to be marked with circumstances of great moral turpitude. The prisoners numbered 130; he passed sentence of death on 29, life transportation on five, 14 years on five, seven years on 11, and various sentences of hard labour on the others.

"The severity of the magistrates at the Quarter Sessions was equally revolting. I notice in one case, where the lead-magistrate on the bench was a great local magnate, an M.P. for Salisbury, a poor fellow with the unfortunate name of Moses Snook was charged with stealing a plank ten feet long, the property of the aforesaid magnate, M.P. etc.; and sentenced to 14 years transportation. Sentenced by the man who owned the plank, worth perhaps a shilling or two."

"The Evening Standard" of March 17th, 1829, gives another sad case from Salisbury Assizes.

"At Salisbury Assizes, Elizabeth Simpson was placed at the bar. Her youthful appearance (being only 17 years of age) her modest demeanour, and the apparent contrition in her mind, excited the sympathy of all who beheld her.

"The facts are that a young lady named Watts had been sent to a school kept by Mrs. Cochrane, of Melksham, to whom the prisoner was assistant. Miss Watts had with her 14 sovereigns, half a sovereign and some silver. Shortly after her arrival they were missing.

After some time the prisoner confessed she had taken the money. When evidence had been given the jury returned a verdict of guilty. Sentence of death was passed."

Sentences passed in the Northern Courts were no more merciful.

"The Doncaster Gazette," of March 24th, 1834, gives the following sentences passed at York Assizes: -

Joseph Senior (30) and John Shaw (39), stealing a horse at Edlington. Transported for life.

John Smith, labourer, for housebreaking at Foggathorpe. Transported for 14 years.

Samuel Kemp and George Vickers, for stealing a sheep at Cusworth, near Doncaster. Transported for life.

"The Daily Independent" of February 27th, 1837, reported that, at Sheffield Intermediate Sessions, John Fitzpatrick, an old offender, was convicted of stealing a shirt from the clothes-lines of Thomas Fido in Wilkinson Street. To be transported for seven years.

The Manchester Justices have recently celebrated the centenary of the grant of a Commission of the Peace to Manchester, and, in the souvenir booklet prepared for that occasion, the first indictment tried at the first Quarter Sessions for the Borough of Manchester, on June 26th, 1839, is given.

The first prisoner mentioned in that indictment was Stephen Forster, a labourer, charged with stealing one hamper of the value of one shilling, two dozen cabbages value one shilling, and two bundles of onions value one shilling. Having been previously convicted at Salford Quarter Sessions, Forster was transported for a term of ten years.

From the "Sunday Times" of March 24th, 1839:-

"Three striking instances of the imperative necessity for a summary and local jurisdiction occured at the Hants Assizes. One was the prosecution of a person for stealing two turnips, the probable value of which did not exceed a penny; another of a woman for stealing a bavin, worth about twopence; and a third of a child of tender years for stealing a few half-pence from his master—to prove which several witnesses were brought from the Isle of Wight!"

Even in those days there were juries and justices humane enough to seek to evade the law, for the benefit of prisoners, although such cases were, unfortunately, all too few.

At one time larceny in a dwelling-house to the value of 40/- or less did not entail the capital penalty, but over 40/- the offender was liable to be sentenced to death.

Lord Holland, speaking in the Lords in 1811, mentioned a case in which a woman was indicted for stealing a ten-pound note in a dwelling house; the note was found upon her, and she assuredly stole that sum or nothing. The jury found her guilty of stealing to the value of 39/-!

The spirit of this jury was also found on occasion, to exist amongst Justices whose sympathies had been aroused by special circumstances in a case before them.

A prisoner was charged with stealing a sheep. Stealing sheep, cattle and horses has always been regarded with peculiar disfavour by the law of England, and, upon such charges prisoners had to be committed for trial. In the case in question, the prisoner was ultimately convicted, summarily, of the offence of stealing a sheepskin, the awkward fact that there had been a live sheep within it at the time it was stolen having, apparently, been overlooked by the Justices!

In another case, Justices convicted a man who had undoubtedly been found in possession of a stolen horse, of the offence of stealing a certain quantity of horsehair.

"At last came the reaction, and the reformers who had been working for years, apparently without avail, now began to make progress, and amazing progress it was. Within 20 years of that time (1810) the practice had grown up of hanging for murder only, and within 50 years (1861) the Consolidation Statutes were passed, when the only capital offences retained upon the Statute-book were murder, treason, piracy with violence, and setting fire to dockyards and arsenals, with the continuance of the practice of hanging for murder only."

In 1784 the procession to Tyburn had been discontinued and the use of the drop to accelerate death by hanging had ben introduced. Public hangings were brought to an end in 1868. The pillory was abolished in 1816, for all offences except perjury, and, finally in 1837. Whipping of females in public had been forbidden in 1791, and, in 1817, all public whippings had to cease. Although pressing to death had long since ceased to be used, the procedure to be adopted when a prisoner refused to plead was finally settled by a statute of 1827. Transportation lasted longer, but came to an end in 1867, and the last record of the stocks being brought into use was in 1872.

DEBTORS' EXERCISE GROUND, NEWGATE GAOL

25

CHAPTER II.

PRISONS OF THE SEVENTEENTH, EIGHTEENTH AND NINETEENTH CENTURIES

"In English law, the prison has always been the King's; yet through all the centuries prior to 1877 it has to be dealt with as part of local government. Though all prisons were, in legal theory, those of the monarch, and though from time immemorial the King's Courts at Westminster had special prisons of their own, up and down the country were other prisons for the maintenance and government of which neither the King, nor any branch of the central administration, made any provision or admitted any responsibility.

"For the safe custody of a person apprehended, the constable was himself responsible, and it had always been left to the parochial or manorial authorities in each place whether or not they would provide a 'cage,' watch house, or temporary 'lock-up.'

"Of common gaols, as distinguished from houses of correction, there seem to have existed, in the sixteenth, seventeenth and eighteenth centuries, up and down the country, something like a couple of hundred.

"The only gaol of which the County Sheriff had the keeping was the county gaol. The towns which were counties ... and practically every corporation, however small, might have its own gaol. Private gaols still existed in the hands of the Bishops and other ecclesiastical potentates, of manorial lords, and other territorial dignitaries, who clung to them as income-yielding properties. (Sidney and Beatrice Webb in "English Prisons Under Local Government.")

This is a true description of the prisons, not only of the sixteenth to the eighteenth centuries but much earlier.

At St. Alban's during Wat Tyler's rebellion in 1381, an attack was made upon the monastery, and the mob commanded the porter to open the gates. "The mob freed *the public malefactors out of the Abbot's prison.*" One of the offenders, whom they supposed unworthy of liberty of life, they beheaded on the ground, before the gate. Here is a case illustrating the use of an ecclesiastical prison for the confinement of public offenders.

A little later, in the reign of the next King, Henry IV., there was an Act (1403-4) directed against the misuse by Constables of Castles, who were also Justices of the Peace, of their castles, and their commissions as Justices, for imprisoning their enemies "They take people, to whom they bear evil will, and imprison them within the said castles, till they have made fine and ransom with the said Constables for their deliverance," and the statute laid down the rule that no Justice of the Peace should imprison, except in the common gaols, but there was a savings clause for the protection of those lords "and others (who have gaols) and their franchises in this case."

A further Act of Henry VII. (1503-4) put all the common gaols under the control and responsibility of the Sheriffs, owing to the many escapes from prison, but exceptions were made in favour of those prisons "whereof any persons spiritual or temporal, or body corporate, have the keeping of estate of inheritance or by succesion" if such prisons were actually being used, and had not fallen into disuse.

Amongst a number of prisons specially exempted from the provisions of the Act were the following:— "A proviso for Henry Wyatt and Thomas Fitzwilliam, the holders of the office of Constable and Porter of Conisborough Castle of Tykhill, part of the Duchy of Lancaster, in Yorkshire."

Prison was, theoretically, a place of detention only, and not of punishment. For felony the punishment was, in general, death. For misdemeanours, the stocks and the pillory, whipping or a fine, were the usual punishments, so that prisons were not the elaborate buildings of to-day. Newgate Prison started with a few dungeons in the old Newgate gateway; the castles of old towns such as Lancaster and York provided cells, or there were dark, noisome cellars under the old Town Halls, or shambles which served the purpose. At Reading three rooms in a public house were devoted to the purposes of a lock-up, and the inn was kept by an old sergeant-at-mace. Many an old mansion had its dark-hole for vagrants and petty offenders, and in many old towns, are still to be seen the lock-ups—small circular buildings of brick or stone—into which the homeless and the "drunks" were thrown for the night.

In the picturesque and ancient gateway of Hooten Pagnell Hall, near Doncaster, there is still the prison-chamber shewn in the illustration on page 8.

It is splendid specimen of the type of cell formerly to be found in many a manorial castle, and has been very little changed since it was first built in early Norman days. The hole in the roof was probably used for the lowering of food and water to the prisoners.

The present Lord of the Manor of Hooton Pagnell (Colonel W. St Andrew Warde-Aldam, D.S.O., D.L., J.P.) kindly gave permission for the flashlight photograph to be taken.

John Howard found that many of the smaller gaols formed the rear of public-houses, the gaoler being the publican. Many more were farmed, and to avoid window tax the gaoler obstructed the light to save his pocket.

The Mayor of Banbury, about the middle of the seventeenth century, confined Anne Audland, a Quakeress, in a filthy place, below ground, with an open sewer running through it, and frogs and toads crawling about the floor. A friend, another Quakeress, who visited there, was seized and imprisoned with her, the two unfortunate women remaining there for seven or eight months.

At Colchester Gaol, the Quaker, James Parnell, was confined in one of a number of holes in the wall, "much like a baker's oven," 12 feet above the ground, the ladder too short by six feet, the remaining six feet being scaled by the aid of a rope. Weakened by illness and hunger, he, at last, fell from the rope and was seriously injured, and taken up for dead, "so they put him in a hole underneath the others, for there were two rows of these holes in the wall." He suffered thus for ten or eleven months, and then fell sick, and died.

The Society of Friends possess many records of the state of the prisons in the seventeenth century, left by those who suffered in them. George Fox was imprisoned in Lancaster Castle, where "the gaoler locked him up in a smoky tower, where one could hardly see a burning candle, so that there seemed an intent to choke him, for the turnkey could hardly be pursuaded to unlock one of the upper doors a little to let the smoke out. Besides this hardship, in the wet weather it rained in upon his bed." When at last he was brought out he was so weak that he could hardly stand or sit on horseback, but he was not allowed any rest, but carried off at once to Scarborough Castle. There he spent fifty shillings to repair the room, to keep out the rain, but was then removed, by the spitefulness of the gaoler, to another room without a chimney or fireplace, so open on the seaward that the rain and spray drove in, and the water ran about the floor and over his bed. In this room he was kept for three months.

Thomas Elwood's diary tells how a jury came to Newgate Prison, to enquire into the death of a prisoner. "As soon as they were come to the door, the foreman, who led them, lifting up his hand, said "Lord bless me, what a sight is here! I did not think there had been so much cruelty in the hearts of Englishmen to use Englishmen in this manner. We need not now question how this man came by his death; we may rather wonder that they are not all dead, for this place is enough to breed an infection amongst them. Well, if it please God to lengthen my life until to-morrow, I will find means to let the King know how his subjects are dealt with."

The sequel to this incident is a very interesting one, for, the next day, the Sheriff came and commanded the removal of the Quaker prisoners to Bridewell. "The porter came to the prisoners and said that, as they knew the way to Bridewell without him, and he could trust them, he should not wait, but would leave them to take their own time, so that they were in before bed-time.

About the middle of the afternoon, therefore, when the streets were full of people, and the shop-keepers standing at the doors, a remarkable procession was to be seen of 32 prisoners, walking two-and-two abreast, with their bundles of clothing on their shoulders, through the Old Bailey into Fleet Street, and so to Bridewell. Several people stopped them to ask who they were, and where they were going, and when they heard that they were prisoners going from Newgate to Bridewell, exclaimed in astonishment, "What, without a keeper?". "No," replied the Friends, "for our word, which we have given, is our keeper."

It was at the time of the Restoration, during the great persecution of the Society, that the "Meeting for sufferings" was formed, to feed and clothe and comfort imprisoned Friends in the prisons and their unfortunate dependents outside. It still forms an important part of the organisation of the Society of Friends.

CARLISLE CASTLE

H. V. Morden, in his graphic style, describes the dungeons in Carlisle Castle:—

"A guide shews you over the keep. He takes you down to the dungeons, and tells you of Bonnie Prince Charlie's rising in 1745. He shews you a small, underground dungeon in which 300 captured Scotsmen were packed tight so that they fought together in the foul darkness to reach the air from the narrow window slits.

"When the gaolers went to this 'Black Hole of Calcutta' in the morning, the dead lay trampled to death beneath the bodies of those who still lived.

"More dramatic, more horrible even than this story, because you can see it, and feel it, is the stone low down in the wall of another dungeon. This cell is underground and has never known daylight. The prisoners had to mount a narrow ledge, some few feet above the level of the floor. There they were manacled, and chained by the neck, so that if they stepped from the ledge they hanged themselves: a release which I suppose many of them welcomed. At certain times they were unchained so that they might walk about. They discovered in this foetid dungeon a stone which was colder than the rest. They must have felt it in the dark. It is still ice-cold. No one knows the reason for this. It seems to sweat frozen moisture. And this stone — I have seen nothing so terrible in any torture chamber — is hollowed out by the fevered tongues of the men once abandoned in this vile hole. Just above it, cut inches deeper in a higher stone, is the shape of a human hand worn in the stone by the fingers of hundreds—thousands—of poor wrethes as they bent down to place their parched tongues to the licking stone.

"High up in the keep of Carlisle Castle, they imprisoned MacDonald of Keppoch, who was captured during the same rising. His little window looked out to Scotland; and the red sandstone is worn an inch deep to the shape of his fingers as he stood there, month after month, gazing hungrily towards the Cheviot hills." Here, too, George Fox was imprisoned in a filthy dungeon amongst the moss-troopers, thieves and murderers. "Yet," he tells in his diary, "bad as the place was, the prisoners were all made very loving and subject to me; and some of them were convinced of the Truth."

GLOUCESTERSHIRE PRISONS

In the year of 1783, the state of the Gloucestershire prisons amounted to a grave public scandal. At the County Gaol in Gloucester City, the whole herd of prisoners, "those committed for trial, and those convicted, the young and the old, are indiscriminately driven at night into one dark pen . . . . A ponderous chain crosses this place of rest, and passing the middle link of each man's fetter, it is made fast at each end, and the whole number are threaded together . . . . There are at present 40 prisoners so threaded together every night." The half dozen little Houses of Correction scattered up and down the county were no less insanitary, whilst they added the additional cruelty of providing no food for their inmates, who were in a state of semi-starvation. The promiscuity and licence which prevailed made the prisons, said the grand jury, "a seminary of vice and a certain introduction to the most infamous practices." Throughout the county Sir George Paul declared, three prisoners died of distemper for every one executed, and of those who died the vast majority were either persons awaiting trial or debtors.

FOOD ALLOWANCES

There was a county allowance for the provision of bread in the county gaols, but it seems impossible to ascertain with any certainty whether, in the smaller gaols, any provision was made for feeding the prisoners, or whether, as in the case of some of the London prisons, they were dependent upon the charity of the philanthropist, or the passer-by who might drop a coin or two into the poor-box outside. In the eighteenth century John Howard found many prisons where the prisoners received no allowance at all, but lived on what they could earn in the prison, the charities of good people, or what they received from their friends.

THE GAOL-FEVER

The lack of even elementary decency led to the strange disease, gaol-fever. John Howard wrote at length condemning the treatment of the prisoners, and the frightful condition of the gaols, which led to frequent outbreaks of this deadly disease. He said, "From my own observations in 1773 and 1774, I was fully convinced that many more were destroyed by it, than were put to death by all the public executions in the kingdom. But the mischief is not confined to prisons—multitudes catch the distemper by going to their relatives and acquaintances in the gaols; many others from prisoners discharged; and not a few in the courts of judicature . . . Even if no mercy were due to the prisoners, the gaol distemper is a national concern of no small importance."

Baker's Chronicle mentions the Assize held at Oxford Castle, 1577, called, from its fatal consequences, "The Black Assize," and records that "all who were present died in 40 hours"; the Lord Chief Baron, the Sheriff, and "about 300 more." In 1730, at the Somerset Assizes, the deadly fever destroyed the Lord Chief Baron and his servants; the High Sheriff and his attendants; many learned Sergeants-at-law and barristers and their clerks; and some hundreds more. In 1750 there was a virulent outbreak amongst those present at the trials at the Old Bailey, and the Lord Mayor, two judges, an alderman, an under-sheriff and 50 others, all perished. Two years later another Lord Mayor contracted the disease and died.

THE PRISON WARDENS

Prison wardens were almost all men who had paid large sums for their positions, and who looked to the prisoners for their incomes, and for the means to replace the capital they had sunk. It is not surprising that the history of prison administration is a dreadful one. Prisoners had but one redress - they could only hope that death would come speedily.

In 1728, public opinion was "greatly stirred" by rumours of terrible happenings in the Fleet and Marshalsea prisons in London. The reports led to the immediate arrest of the Wardens, charged with murder and robbery with violence . . . One man had given £5,000 for the wardenship of the Fleet Prison, and he sold it for the same amount. He and his deputy were put upon their trial for the ghastly happenings in the prison. Both were acquitted by the jury. A man named Acton was brought to trial upon four charges of murder at the Marshalsea. He, too, was acquitted. The Judge refused to accept the verdicts, and a fifth bill of indictment was thrown out by the Grand Jury. So much for that "public feeling" which had been so "greatly stirred," and so much for the London prisons. That men had been manacled, tortured, confined in fearsome dens and holes, starved, and eventually done to death was agreed by all, save the accused, but such was the state of public opinion of that duty—so brutalised, so intimidated by cruelties, and so habituated to grievous wrongs—that it was impossible to find a jury courageous enough to convict the murderers. A century and a half had yet to pass before the evils of the English prison system were finally to be ended.

At Newgate, amongst the thousand evils which flourished unchecked, there was one which, even to-day, stirs us to anger. Prior to 1430, there had been no water supply to the prison, and it was to relieve this grave hardship that a kindly Lord Mayor of London, one Thomas Knowles, a grocer, had a pipe laid which conveyed water from the cistern of his own house to the suffering prisoners. For two centuries after this there were constant complaints, only too true, that the gaolers suffered the precious water to reach those for whom it had been provided only on payment of exhorbitant charges.

Many prisoners, acquitted of the charges made against them, and entitled to be released, were carried back to the gaols because they were unable to pay the gaolers' fees. It was not until 1774 that this evil was ended by Act of Parliament, and, even after that date, John Howard made the discovery that, although cleared of gaolers' fees, acquitted prisoners were still subject to a similar demand made by Clerks of Assize and Clerks of the Peace, and that men who should have been free were being detained in prisons for several days after their acquittals by these officials. "I was informed at Durham" (wrote John Howard) "that Judge Gold, at the Assizes held there in 1775, laid a fine of £50 upon the gaoler for detaining some acquitted prisoners for fees due to the Clerk of Assize, but, upon the intercession of the Bishop *(the proprietor of the gaol)* the fine was remitted and the prisoners set at large."

THE HULKS

In 1779, the American Civil War broke out, and, owing to the enforced and sudden stoppage of the transportation of criminals to North America, the Government was brought face to face with the duty of establishing and maintaining prisons. As over a thousand criminals were being evacuated annually from the country at this time, the problem was a very urgent one. An attempt was made to force the Justices into a scheme for enlarging the local prisons, but the weight of their opinion was against the Government, and it was then decided to utilise the old war-vessels as "hulks" for temporarily confining prisoners awaiting transportation, and two old ships were hurriedly converted to this purpose. Later, additional hulks were provided in the Thames and Medway, and at Portsmouth Harbour.

The history of the hulks proves conclusively that the experiment—at first, a temporary one, but destined to last for eighty years—was one of the most unsuccessful ever attempted in the long and evil history of English prison administration. "Of all places of confinement that British history records, the hulks were apparently the most brutalising, the most demoralising, and the most horrible. The death rate was appalling, even for the prisons of the period. Though the convicted had the advantage of working in the open air, the cruelties to which they were subjected by day, and the horrors of their association by night, make the record one of the very blackest" (Sidney and Beatrice Webb).

Another writer says: "They were dirty, crowded and verminous, with the men and boys all in irons, often in double irons, for greater security. The prisoners were sadly neglected. Upon the hospital ship at Woolwich, for instance, neither towels nor even combs were provided, and most of the patients were infested with vermin. Some of the sick, especially if insane, lay in a horrible condition of filth and wretchedness. The senior medical officer of the hulks on the Thames had a private practice; the assistant surgeon was not a qualified man at all, but a medical student. Among the criminals, lunatics, and outcasts of all kinds cooped up for periods generally ranging from one year to seven years, were young boys. An old table gives the number on the hulks at one time—a child of two, two of 12, four of 14, and altogether 20 boys of less than 16 years old. On the hulk Euryalus, the youngest villain was nine years old. Some of the boys, the inspector reported, were so young they could hardly put their clothes on.

Those who were able to do rough work were employed on shore on dockyard tasks, such as digging and dredging. They were allowed some beer, and when they got back to the ship in the evening they were allowed some freedom (in spite of their fetters, and a little tobacco with which to console themselves, but there prevailed the usual stagnation of prison life, particularly for those who were unable to go on shore. There was bad language, some pilfering, and occasional violence, both by convicts and overseers. The convicts were liable to be flogged with a severe sort of cat, to the extent of two dozen lashes. There were a great number of feeble degenerates, including some dazzled by solitary confinement in the prisons on shore, and there were many lunatics, who were often troublesome and were often flogged like the other captives."

(George Ives in "A History of Penal Methods")

The Act of 1779, passed to deal with the emergency, provided that the hulks were "for the more severe and effectual punishment of atrocious and daring

KIRKBY MALZEARD CELLS

MODERN CELLS (STAINFORTH, YORKS)

offenders," so that the men were, in the main, hardened and dangerous criminals. The Act provided that they should be employed in raising sand, soil and gravel from the River Thames and other navigable rivers, and they also gave some assistance under guard, in the dockyards. After transportation was resumed, to the newly-discovered continent of Australia, to Tasmania, and Norfolk Island, the rate of transportation to the new penal colonies failed to overtake the flow of men to the hulks. From the time of the first shipment to New South Wales (in 1787) down to the last, to the Swan River (in 1867) something like 150,000 convicts must have been poured into the three colonies, a large proportion of whom never returned to England. In spite of this flow of human beings from England, an average of nearly 2,000 a year, there were still 3,550 convicts on board the various hulks in England in 1841. In one hulk in 1841, there were 638 convicts; 400 were in hospital and 38 deaths occurred. The hulks were rotten and leaky, overrun by rats, cockroaches and other vermin, and cholera and other diseases took such a toll of the unhappy men that large numbers never left the hulks to serve their sentences abroad, but died on the ships.

A note in the "Observer" of June 12th, 1836, seems to suggest that women, as well as men, were kept on these hulks, whilst awaiting transportation:—

"Yesterday morning 25 female convicts were conveyed from Newgate to the hulk moored off Woolwich, preparatory to their transmission to New South Wales, to which colony the major part of them are banished for 14 years, and some for the term of their natural lives.

By a recent regulation of the Government, the female convicts, should their conduct warrant it, will be placed in domestic situations suitable to their abilities."

HOUSES OF CORRECTION

The development of the local "houses of correction" or "bridewells" (first established as workhouses for vagrants and the unemployed, under the direct supervision of the Justices), into a form of prison had, in the meantime been proceeding with some rapidity, and these houses of correction were used more and more for the confinement of petty offenders, until in 1720, the change in their character and purposes was confirmed by an Act of Parliament, and they became ordinary prisons.

It was in those prisons that, early in the nineteenth century, the question arose as to the practice of the Justices, (or, at any rate, with their consent) of causing untried prisoners to work, limiting the alternatives to bread and water on the one hand, or the treadmill on the other.

Some facts are available as to the conditions in the Wakefield House of Correction, which afford a general idea as to later developments in this type of prison.

WAKEFIELD HOUSE OF CORRECTION

The Wakefield House of Correction was a typical establishment of this kind, originally established in order to provide work for the poor, but gradually absorbed into the prison system of the county, until it became the principal prison for the West Riding. By the will of Mr. George Savile of Wakefield, gentleman, dated December 16th, 1594, the first gift was made—"I give twenty pounds for and towards the building of an House of Correction within seven miles of Wakefield for the setting of the poor to work, or towards a stock for keeping of them in works according to the statute, if there be any such house builded within two years after my decease, and, if there be not, then this bequest utterly to be void."

In 1576, the counties had been required to provide and maintain "Abiding Houses or Houses of Correction," in which sturdy beggars, rogues and vagabonds were "to be as straitly kept in diet as in work." The Houses of Correction (of which there were ultimately about 200) were under the absolute control of the Justices in Quarter Sessions. "So little at the outset were these places regarded as places of punishment, and so much as means of finding employment for the unemployed poor, that it was evidently not unusual, about the middle of the seventeenth century, to give the inmates regular wages in return for their work." There is a good deal of evidence that, in the early days, these Houses of Correction or Bridewells carried out good work, under careful supervision as to cleanliness, discipline and diet, and that, as they were gradually absorbed into the ordinary prison system they deteriorated to the abject level of that system. Sixty years after its opening the Wakefield House of Correction was already in a ruinous state, though full of prisoners, and the records of Quarter Sessions shew great concern at its decay. In 1682 the governor was reimbursed certain sums expended by him "in keeping felons which have been committed to him which ought by law to have been sent to the common gaol," and shortly after this date he complained that "he had 30 felons committed to the said house lately." A claim by the same governor in 1690 mentions 67 felons committed to his charge. In view of complaints by the governor that the House of Correction was overcrowded with felons, it is surprising that, at Wakefield sessions in 1689 the Justices agreed to allow certain rooms to be used as a common workhouse, for setting the poor to work. What success attended this experiment is not recorded.

John Howard's report upon the Wakefield House of Correction (1773-75) was not an enthusiastic one: "This prison is unfortunately built upon low ground; it is damp and exposed to floods. Four of the wards are spacious; but all the wards are made very offensive by sewers, and are dark. Prison and court out of sight from the keeper's house: some prisoners have escaped. They are now let out to the court only half an hour a day. The wards are dirty . . . Allowance 2d. per day; little or no employment."

That prisoners had escaped, and that Governor Waugh was not free from blame, is proved by a record of the prison (1767-9) which states that the governor was fined £20 on January 12th, 1769, for allowing a woman to escape. The fine, however, was remitted in the following April.

In 1791, in a sudden accession of energy, the Justices discovered that much was wrong in the gaol—"the Justices having inspected Mr. Waugh's accounts do find that his account of the earnings of the prisoners is imaginary. It is, therefore, ordered that in future he do keep a true account of the prisoner's earnings."

The same year, there were further discoveries by the Justices—"This Court upon examination into the state of the House of Correction finds with great surprise and concern that, notwithstanding the great expense bestowed upon the same, the regulations that have been made, and the large allowance to the Governor, great abuses prevail there which require immediate regulation." For the first time provision was to be made for a room in which Divine service could be held; a male and a female overlooker were appointed to supervise the work of the prisoners; felons were to be kept away from other prisoners. In 1807, the Government Inspector discovered that Joseph Scott, the gaoler, kept the adjoining public house, the Duke of Leeds' Arms! By the beginning of the nineteenth century the influence of John Howard was beginning to be felt in most of the county gaols and the Houses of Correction, and the tremendous task of reform had begun. The history of the Wakefield House of Correction both before and after this period is identical with the history of a hundred other such gaols. Corruption and cruelty were discovered from time to time, and dealt with; governors and turnkeys were removed from their offices; twice in the first half of the nineteenth century cholera swept through many prisons (including Wakefield); prisoners still died of gaol-fever, and want and misery; but the leaven of reform was at work, and the worst days were over.

PUBLIC EXHIBITIONS

Outside the prisons the nation shewed little sign that opinion was turning against public exhibitions of cruelty, such as executions, the exposure of criminals in the pillory, the whippings through the street. The body of Mary Bateman, executed at York on March 20th, 1809, was given to the authorities at Leeds Infirmary, who allowed 2,500 persons to see it on payment of 3d. each. "The body was then dissected" (the grisly record relates), "her skin was tanned and distributed." It is not surprising that, when such an appalling exhibition could attract 2,500 of the people of Leeds, the work of the reformer made but slow progress.

NUMBERS IN THE PRISONS

How many persons were in the English prisons in any given year it is impossible to say. So many prisoners were disposed of by the pillory or whipping, transporting and hanging, and the burning in the hand of those who obtained the benefit of clergy, that those left in the gaols were kept down to (a) debtors, (b) those awaiting trial for felony, (c) those awaiting trial or serving sentences for misdemeanours, (d) those committed for failing to find sureties. John Howard estimated the total number in 1779 at 4,375, of whom nearly half were debtors. Certainly no one in England had more knowledge and experience upon which to form an estimate than John Howard, but in view of figures available at the beginning of the next century, his estimate seems very low. It is clear, however, that there was a great increase towards the end of the eighteenth century, and during the first years of the nineteenth century, in the numbers found in prison. For instance, the Wakefield House of Correction had 238 committals in 1779 (the year quoted by Howard), but this number had increased to 642 in 1809, and 20 years later, in 1829, to 2,844 persons.

The Gentleman's magazine, in 1759, in the course of an article on the prisons, declared that "The heaviness of sorrow; the confined air, want of exercise, and, sometimes of food; the contagion of diseases from which there is no retreat, and the severity of tyrants, against whom there can be no resistance, and all the complicated horrors of a prison, put an end every year to the life of one in four of those thus shut up from the common comforts of life. Thus perish yearly 5,000 men, overborne with sorrow, consumed by famine, many of them in the most vigorous and useful part of life."

This statement, taken literally, implies that 20,000 persons went through the prisons each year, of whom 5,000 died in confinement, and this may be taken to confirm, in some degree, John Howard's estimate of just under 5,000 prisoners at a given time each year.

SILENCE IN THE PRISONS

The law of silence in the prisons may be said to have been one of the marked changes in the administration of the prisons. In the eighteenth century, and earlier, prisoners were allowed to—were in fact compelled to—herd together in an extraordinary way. Nearly all the prisoners were ironed, so that there was little chance of escape, and, to give one illustraion only of the absence of any classification or segregation of prisoners, it is a fact that even the condemned were, in some prisons, left to mix with the crowd of prisoners until required by the executioner. But there was no law of silence; in fact, one of the things which impressed the early reformers most was the filthy nature of the conversations overheard, the obscene language and the perpetual pandemonium which reigned.

In the nineteenth century there grew up the custom of enforcing silence in the prisons; men and women lived, and worked, and fed, and slept in an unnatural and unnerving silence. It was the longing of the prisoners to speak, and to be spoken to, which led to more breaches of discipline in the nineteenth century prison, and more punishments, than any other type of offence. Since 1898, there has been no "law of silence," strictly so-called. Previously to that date the order ran, "The Governor shall enforce the observance of silence throughout the prison." A Committee which sat in 1894 reported that "We think that the privilege of talking might be given after a certain period as a reward for good conduct, *on certain days for a given time* . . . The present practice of imposing silence, except for the purposes of labour and during the visits of officials and authorised persons, for a period of 15 to 20 years, seems to us unnatural."

At Cold Baths Prison even the treadmill was so partitioned off that each prisoner toiled up the endless ascent in silence, and alone.

MASKED PRISONERS

An addition to the horrors of perpetual silence, inflicted in some of the prisons, was that of masking the prisoners. Pentonville Prison, constructed in 1842 as a "model" prison, dealt with first offenders between 18 and 35 years of age. For 18 months these unfortunate men lived in complete isolation, so complete that masks were worn to avoid recognition. Even service at Chapel was arranged on a separate system, each prisoner being placed in a small cubicle from which he could not see his fellow-prisoners.

At Wandsworth Prison, opened in 1851, there was the same enclosed pew system in chapel as at Pentonville, despite the wishes of the inspectors of prisons and the clergy, that the system should be abolished. A mask covered the face, having eyelet holes. A piece of alpaca cloth was inserted over the mouth for freer respiration. The prisoners were then unmasked in chapel, and in their cells. The women wore alpaca veils.

One writer says: "The prisoners have an envious and sinister appearance as they look at us with hasty stolen glance through the eyelet openings in their masks, as at Pentonville." The problem of finding a middle course between the promiscuity of the eighteenth century, and the cruel silence of the nineteenth century, has been one which has led to many experiments in the present century, but the immorality and degradation of the earlier period, and the demoralising rigidity and discipline of the last century, have both given way to an earnest effort to find a compromise between the two methods.

UNTRIED PRISONERS

Here is a description of the treatment of untried prisoners, which the Quaker, Sir Thomas Fowell Buxton, saw with his own eyes in 1818, in the prisons administered by the Middlesex Quarter Sessions and the Corporation of the City of London. "The prisoner, after his commitment is made out, is handcuffed to a file of perhaps a dozen wretched persons in a similar situation and marched through the streets, sometimes a considerable distance, followed by a crowd of impudent and insulting boys; the moment he enters prison irons are hammered on him; then he is cast into the midst of a compound of all that is disgusting and depraved. At night he is locked up in a narrow cell with perhaps half a dozen of the worst thieves in London, or as many vagrants, whose rags are alive and in actual motion with vermin; he may find himself in bed, and in bodily contact, between a robber and a murderer; or between a man with a foul disease on one side and one with an infectious disorder on the other. He may spend his days deprived of free air and wholesome exercise . . . He may be half starved for want of food and clothing and fuel . . . His trial may be long and protracted; he may be imprisoned on suspicion and pine in gaol while his family is starving out of it, without any opportunity of removing that suspicion, and for a whole year. If acquitted he may be dismissed from the gaol without a shilling in his pocket, and without the means of returning home."

Nor were untried prisoners treated any more considerately in the provinces. In 1822 it was the practice in the West Riding "for the prisoners . . . to be marched from Wakefield to the place where the Court is to sit, chained two together by their necks, besides the usual handcuffs on their wrists; in this way they are marched sometimes to Skipton, nearly 35 miles; to Knaresborough 25 miles, and other places of shorter distance, to take their trial. The exposure of 50 or 60 prisoners on the high roads in these populous districts is certainly a great evil as regards the prisoner himself, who is not yet proved guilty." Not until 1823 did any local authorities convey untried prisoners in the decent seclusion of a covered van; and when in that year the Surrey Justices introduced this reform, their example was not followed even by the Middlesex Justices for four years. It was not until 1827, too, that the West Riding Justices gave up marching their prisoners on foot from town to town, and provided a covered van for their conveyance. (The practice of handcuffing a number of prisoners to a long chain for the purpose of taking then to and from the railway stations lasted until well into the present century in the West Riding—probably in many other places also. I remember seeing twenty-three prisoners, sentenced, or on remand, handcuffed to a long chain, marched from the Police Station to the railway station, en route to Wakefield Prison. One reason for the custom was, of course, the great saving in the number of police officers required as escort).

POLICE CELLS

Police station cells have, for many years now, been built on more or less stereotyped lines, giving the maximum of light and air, efficient sanitary and washing arrangements, scrupulous cleanliness and effective supervision. The illustration on page 34 of modern cells (at Stainforth near Doncaster) gives a glimpse of cells recently constructed on these lines.

The cells in the older police stations, though actually not quite so up-to-date are usually somewhat similar in construction. It is surprising to find that the cells at Kirkby Malzeard, near Ripon, built about 1866, are really cages, with strong iron bars an inch thick. Each cell has a large iron gate, with heavy iron clasps at the top and bottom, and two large padlocks. Inside each cage is a wooden bed, six feet eight inches long, by three feet four inches wide. Whatever complaints prisoners may have made against these curious cells, they could not complain of lack of ventilation!

The cages were last used some years ago.

CHAPTER III.

CHILDREN AND PUNISHMENT

"To sit and bask in the sunshine of the eighteenth century, with Austin Dobson turning on the sun, is a rare and holy joy," said Sir Walter Besant. There was little sunshine in the lives of many children in the eighteenth century, and there is small cause for holy joy, apart from the pleasure of reading Austin Dobson's calm and reflective prose, in his description of the origin of the Foundling Hospital.

("Captain Coram's Charity" Series I. of Eighteenth Century Vignettes.)

It is impossible, in a brief chapter, to give more than a hint of the treatment of little children in past centuries, but this essay casts an unpleasant light upon the heartlessness and cold cruelty with which helpless infants were viewed in the eighteenth century.

Captain Thomas Coram, an old sea captain, and a great-hearted kindly man, engaged in much good work, but his crowning philanthropy was the obtaining of a charter for the establishment of the Foundling Hospital. Going to and fro, "he was constantly coming upon half-clad infants, sometimes alive, sometimes dead, and sometimes dying, who had been abandoned by their parents to the mercy of the streets," and he determined to find an asylum for these helpless, abandoned babes. His campaign lasted 17 years, and ended in the foundation of the Foundling Hospital, but immediately his good work began to be abused. Consigning children to the hospital was an easy way of disposing of them, and it became a lucrative trade to convey infants from remote country places to the hospital.

"Once a waggoner brought eight to town, seven of whom were dead when they reached their destination.

"On another occasion a man with five in baskets got drunk on the road, and three of his charges were suffocated.

"The inevitable outcome of this was that the Governors discovered very speedily that they were admitting far more inmates than they could possibly afford to maintain.

"They accordingly applied to Parliament, who voted them £10,000, but at the same time crippled them with the obligation to receive all comers.

"A basket was forthwith hung at the gate, with the result that, on the first day of its appearance, no less than 117 infants were successfully deposited in it.

"That this extraordinary development of the intentions of the projectors could continue to work satisfactorily was, of course, impossible, and great mortality ensued.

"As time went on, however, a wise restriction prevailed, and the Hospital now exists solely for those unmarried mothers whose previous character has been good, and whose desire to reform is believed to be sincere."

Doubtless the merciless treatment of unmarried mothers by Quarter Sessions—the flogging of the mothers and the forcing of the mothers and babes on to the roads to return to their places of settlement—accounts in some measure for this extraordinary experience of the Foundling Hospital, but the story sheds a terrible light upon the attitude of men and women towards these helpless infants, an attitude which found expression, also, in the treatment of the unfortunate children who transgressed any of the multitude of cruel and savage laws of the time, and their stolid acquiescence in the horrible sentences passed upon them.

Until well into the nineteenth century the treatment of children in the courts differed in no degree from that meted out to adult criminals. Although there were, even in those dark days, some kindly people who pleaded for mercy and sympathy to be extended to the younger offenders, the policy of savage punishments to which the nation had been so long accustomed continued to be applied to even the children. Judges and Justices who may have been, in their private lives, affectionate and considerate parents, passed upon the wrteched children brought before them sentences which horrify us to-day.

On February 24th, 1732, at the Old Bailey, 54 persons were sentenced, ten of them to be hanged. Amongst the ten sentenced to death was George Dawson, described as "a little boy," who had stolen from a shop 20 pairs of children's stockings, valued at 5/6, and a wollen petticoat.

William West, aged 16, was another of those sentenced to death, for burglary.

Of the remaining 44 persons convicted, one was sentenced to be burnt on the hand, and 43 to be transported to the colonies.

George Dawson was reprieved later though what alternative sentence was passed upon him is not known, but the youth William West, and all the other eight offenders, were duly hanged outside Newgate gaol.

The case of William York, aged 10, tried at Bury Assizes in 1748, is reported in Foster's Crown Cases.

The boy murdered a small girl of five, with a knife, and buried her body. The Judges who tried him were reluctant to believe in "his mischievous discretion," and the execution was respited until the Judges had conferred. By a majority they decided that the boy ought to be put to death, but there were other reprieves until, at last the sentence was confirmed. The Secretary of State then intervened, and reprieved the boy, but he was kept in prison for nine years, and then, when a young man of 19, he was pardoned on condition that he joined the navy.

In the Sessions Papers (Old Bailey) of the year 1804, Case N. 200 is reported as follows: -

"George Atwell (aged 14) was indicted for burglariously breaking and entering the dwelling-house of Thomas Revill, about the hour of 8 p.m., on the 1st of February, with intent to steal, and feloniously stealing therin, three pairs of steel snuffers, value 4/-, and three Japan snuffer-trays, value 3/-, the property of Thomas Revill.

"Evidence was called to prove the taking of the property through a broken shop window, which had been temporarily repaired with putty.

"Verdict: Guilty. Sentence: Death."

The prison chaplains in those days were frequently men of low character, self-indulgent and utterly regardless of the moral obligations of their high calling. A committee, appointed in 1814, reported upon the chaplain at Newgate in these words: "Beyond his attendance in chapel and on those who are sentenced to death, Dr. Forde feels but few duties to be attached to his office. He knows nothing of the state of morals in the prison; he never sees any of the prisoners in private; though 14 boys and girls between nine and 13 years of age were in Newgate in April last, he does not consider attention to them a point of his duty; he never knows that they have been sick until he gets a warning to attend their funeral; he does not go to the infirmary, for it is not in his instructions."

This particular man of God received £300 a year and perquisites.

In 1833 a child of nine was sentenced to death at the Old Bailey for stealing goods worth 2d. and confined to the condemned cells at Newgate until the Recorder's report had been sent to the Secretary of State and the reprieve had arrived, after the usual delays.

W. Eden Hooper, in "Newgate and the Old Bailey," tells a pitiful story of the condition of the children.

"Until well into Queen Victoria's reign the law had little thought for the children. They were accustomed to see infamous scenes in public places— hangings, whippings, and the torture of the pillory. They were themselves whipped in public for begging and wandering. The fact that they had no food and no shelter was not considered. The law robbed them of their natural protectors by executing them and transporting them . . . It was no uncommon sight to see a woman carted to the gallows with a baby at her breast, and older ones clinging to her to the last. It awoke no thought of pity in official places. The children were forthwith taken before a magistrate for 'instruction.' If they were of very tender years they were given into the 'care' of the beadle of the parish. If they were old enough to work, they were bound to the service of anyone who expressed himself willing to take them. Taking children off the hands of the parish and making them work night and day until they died under their labour was a common and recognised practice up to the end of the first quarter of the nineteenth century. Then the Press took the matter up; a great public scandal resulted, and the homeless, starving and defenceless children received a little more consideration . . .

"I ought to mention that mothers cast for transportation were allowed to take their younger children with them, the age limit being about eight years for boys and 10 or 11 for girls."

So late as 1850, Tothill Fields Prison, the Middlesex House of Correction, was reserved for the reception of women and boys under 17, there being accommodation for 300 boys.

Albert Crew, in "London Prisons," says that "The juvenile offenders were much more difficult to manage than the adults, or else they were more tyrannically treated by their gaolers, for the number of punishments meted out to them was more than double those inflicted upon the adult prisoners, 11 per cent. of the boys being placed in the dark cells.

43

"One of the prolific cases of the great number of juvenile offenders imprisoned here was the fact that children were sentenced for the most trivial offences.

"In 1851-2, 55 children under 14 years of age were committed to prison for stealing articles under the value of 6d. and 136 for stealing goods under the value of 2/6. Naturally the effect on the juvenile prisoner of imprisonment for such offences developed a recklessness of character which led to the committal of greater crime. There were usually some 2,500 boys under 17 committed every year to this prison, of whom 200 had been committed four times or more."

To us to-day the revelation of the legal murders and cruelties connected with the trial of children are revolting. We have become so habituated to the kindly and even anxious atmosphere of the Children's Courts, that it is hard to believe that the full ceremonial, the dread ordeal, of the assize Courts could have been brought into use against little children of seven years and upwards—judges uttering their cruel legal platitudes; the chaplain sitting by assenting; the Sheriff in his impressive uniform; ladies coming to the Court to be entertained by such a sight—the spectacle of a terrified little child about to receive the death sentence which the verdict of 12 men, probably fathers of families themselves, had given the judge power to pass.

Later on the intervening Sunday before the execution took place, the child, with the other condemned, sat in the railed-off enclosure in the centre of the chapel at Newgate, a minister of God preached the death sermon - for money; and "ladies" and "gentlemen" filled the public gallery as spectators.

The late Mr. Waddy, a Metropolitan magistrate, in his book, "The Police Court and its Work," says: "The old Sessions papers are the reports of proceedings in criminal cases tried at the Old Bailey. You may take at random any volume, say, between the years 1800 and 1825, and find with certainty the record of some young person under sixteen years receiving sentence of death or transportation for some trivial offence which, in modern days, would be punished by some small fine, or dealt with under the Probation Act."

How differently the State regards the juvenile offender now is shewn by the fact that the above words are quoted in the Report of the Children's Branch of the Home Office, and that the following sentences follow the quotation:-

"The author of 'Old Bailey Experiences' (printed in 1833) says: "Nothing can be more absurd than the passing of sentences of death on boys under 14 years of age for petty offences. I have known five in one session in this awful situation; one for stealing a comb almost valueless, two for a child's sixpenny story-book, another for a man's stock, and the fifth for pawning his mother's shawl. In four of these cases the boys put their hands through a broken pane of glass in a shop window and stole the articles for which they were sentenced to death, and, subsequently transported for life. This act, in legal technicality, is housebreaking.

'In 1838 the boys' prison at Parkhurst was established, to which boys under 16, sentenced to transportation, were sent, and even there they were guarded by warders with fixed bayonets. Not long afterwards, under the influence of Mathew Davenport Hill and Mary Carpenter, the first of the Reformatory

SANCTUARY CHAIR, SPOTBOROUGH CHURCH, NEAR DONCASTER

BEVERLEY MINSTER (Original site of Fridstool marked with X)

Schools was established. The modern system of treatment for young delinquents, of which the juvenile Court as we know it to-day is the outcome, may be said to have begun at the middle of the nineteenth century.'" (1928 Report).

Even so late as 1847, the Juvenile Offenders Act of that year illustrates the grudging spirit in which concessions were made to the growing spirit of hostility which was being manifested all over England against cruel sentences on children. This Act (quoting the preamble) was pased

"To ensure the more speedy trial of juvenile offenders under 14 and to *avoid the evils of their long imprisonment previously to trial.*"

The Act was applied to larceny, and cases punishable as simple larceny only.

The punishments, given to the justices to administer were:-

Imprisonment for three months.
Fine of £3.
Whipping.

Then follows this remarkable instance of legal injustice:-

"Provided that, if such Justices *shall deem the offence not proved,* or not expedient to inflict any punishment, they shall dismiss the party charged *on finding surety or sureties for his good behaviour.*"

And presumably, if the child could not find the necessary sureties (although not guilty of the offence) he could be sent to prison in default.

In the remarkable book written by Henry Mayhew and John Binny, "Criminal Prisons of London," published in 1862, there are some pitiful facts with regard to youthful "criminals" of that time.

"Those who have never looked into the matter will, doubtless, be startled to learn that the average number of juvenile prisoners annually passing through the gaols of the entire country amounts to no less than 11,749 . . .

"One prolific cause of the increase of juvenile offenders is the fact that children are sent to prison for the most trivial offences . . .

"In the oakum-room, at Tothill Fields prison, there were altogether 150 or more children congregated together. Some had large figures 1 or 2, in yellow cloth, on their arms, to denote the class to which they belonged. The first-class prisoners had more than three months imprisonment to undergo, while the second-class prisoners were under imprisonment for three months . . . Others, again, had badges showing that they were imprisoned for two years; others had a yellow ring on the left arm, to denote that their sentence was penal servitude.

"It was a melancholy sight to look at that century and a half of mere children in their prison clothes. Some were so young they seemed to need a nurse, rather than a gaoler, to look after them; others, again had such frank innocent-looking faces that we could not help fancying they had no business to be there . . .

"We know of no sight in London so terribly pathetic if not tragic—as this same oakum-room at the boys' prison at Westminster . . . True, the place is called a house of correction; rightly viewed, it is simply a criminal preparatory school. Here we find little creatures of six years of age branded with a felon's badge - boys, not even in their 'teens, clad in the prison dress, for their heinous offences of throwing stones, or obstructing highways, or unlawfully knocking at doors . . .

"If it were not for the pathos of the place, we could really believe this boys' prison would rank as the great laughing-stock of the age, for here one finds all the pompous paraphenalia of Visiting Justices, and Governors and Warders, with bunches of keys dangling from thick chains, and strings of cutlasses hanging over the mantel-piece of the entrance office—all to take care of the little desperate malefactors, not one of whom has cut his wisdom teeth, whilst many are so young they seem better fitted to be conveyed to the prison in a perambulator than in the lumbering and formidable prison van.

"Standing within the prison gateway was a man whose heavy boots were yellow with dry clay, and whose plush waistcoat gave signs of his being some navvy or brickmaker. The man touched his fur cap as we passed and hoped we would help him with a trifle to carry him and his boy (who was about to be liberated) towards Enfield. The child was eight years old, we learnt. His offence had been stealing some half-dozen plums from an orchard—his sentence 14 days and a flogging.

"Later we accompanied the warder to the exercise yard . . . One of the lads, who had been ten times recommitted, was called out of the ranks and questioned.

"'How old are you?'
"'Thirteen years, please, sir.'
"'What are you in for?'
"'Coat and umbrella, sir. This makes seven times here, three times at Coldbaths Prison.'
"'How long have you got now?'
"'Three months. This makes four times, please sir, that I've had three calendar months, and I've had two monthses as well.'

"On one of the days of our inspection of this prison, three fresh prisoners had arrived; two wretched, shoeless, and ragged creatures, one more decently clad, his darned clothes telling that he, at least, had a mother who took some care of him. The latter boy had, we were told, just been sent from the sessions; he was 13 years old and had got two years' imprisonment for stealing brass."

Such was the treatment given to children in the year 1862. To-day no child under eight can be charged with a criminal offence; a sentence of death cannot be passed upon a person under 18 years of age; a child cannot be sent to imprisonment or penal servitude, nor can a young person between 14 and 17 be sent to prison, except under certain special circumstances. Committal for trial, so far as children between eight and 14 are concerned, is at an end, with one possible exception.

So, in the space of a few years, enlightenment has come, and the evils of centuries, suddenly seen in their true horror and disgrace, have been abolished.

And society to-day, by voluntary effort, now tries to make amends for the unspeakable brutalities meted out to children in past centuries by supporting Children's Homes and Orphanages, Children's Hospitals, splendid societies, such as the National Society for the Prevention of Cruelty to Children, Children's Camps, and a thousand and one other proofs that the old days, so far as children are concerned, have for ever passed away.

For a juvenile wrong-doer, the new spirit is demonstrated by the Children's Courts and Remand Homes, Home Office Schools, a great probation system, the machinery of education and a humane poor-law system, and many other thoughtful experiments in child-reformation. These have taken the place of evil and insanitary prisons, the whipping-post, the gallows, irons, the stocks, transportation, and the other symbols of the law a century ago.

CHAPTER IV.

OUTLAWRY.

"The daylight had dawned upon the glades of the oak forest. The green boughs glittered with all their pearls of dew. The hind led her fawn from the covert of high fern to the more open walks of the greenwood, and no huntsman was there to watch or interrupt the stately hart, as he paced at the head of the antlered herd.

"The outlaws were all assembled around the Trysting tree in the Harthill walk, where they had spent the night in refreshing themselves after the fatigues of the siege, some with wine, some with slumber, many with hearing and recounting the events of the day, and computing the heaps of plunder which their success had placed at the disposal of their chief.

"The spoils were indeed very large; for notwithstanding that much was consumed, a great deal of plate, rich armour, and splendid clothing had been secured by the exertions of the dauntless outlaws, who could be appalled by no danger when such rewards were on view. Yet so strict were the laws of their society, that no one ventured to appropriate any part of the booty, which was brought into one common mass, to be at the disposal of their leader.

"The place of rendezvous was an aged oak . . . Here Locksley assumed his seat—a throne of turf erected under the twisted branches of the huge oak, and the sylvan followers were gathered around him."

Such is the picture drawn of Robin Hood, most famous of outlaws, and his band, by the romantic pen of Sir Walter Scott in "Ivanhoe"; sunshine, the beauty of the forest, freedom, fearlessness and spoil.

The picture sketched by Sir Conan Doyle in "The White Company" of the death of outlaws in the New Forest is not so alluring.

"Down the slanting road there was riding a big burly man, clad in a tunic of purple velvet, and driving a great black horse as hard as it could gallop ... Behind him rode six others, two and two, clad in sober brown jerkins, with the long yellow staves of their bows thrusting out from behind the right shoulders. Down the hill they thundered, over the brook and up to the scene of the contest.

"'Here is one,' said the leader, springing down from his reeking horse, and seizing the white rogue by the edge of his jerkin, 'I know him by the devil's touch upon his brow. Where are your cords Peterkin? Go! bind him hand and foot. His last hour has come . . . But there should be another one, a black man. Leave that rogue lying. Now stretch out my line, my merry ones, with arrow on string, and I shall show you such sport as only a king can give. Beat high and low among the heather, and a pot of wine to the lucky marksman.'

"As it chanced, however, the searchers had not far to seek. The negro had burrowed down into his hiding place upon the barrow, where he might have lain snug enough, had it not been for the red gear upon his head. As he raised himself to look over the bracken at his enemies, the staring colour caught the eye of the bailiff, who broke into a long screeching whoop, and spurred forward sword in hand. Seeing himself discovered, the man rushed from his hiding-place, and bounded at top speed, keeping a good hundred paces in front of them. The two who were on either side of Alleyne bent their bows as calmly as though they were shooting at the popinjay at a village fair.

"'Seven yards windage, Hal,' said one whose hair was streaked with grey. 'Five,' replied the other, letting loose his string. The yellow streak seemed to pass right through the man, but he still ran forward.

"'Seven, you jack-fool,' growled the first speaker, and his bow twanged like a harp-string. The black man sprang high up into the air, and shot out both his arms and legs, coming down all asprawl among the heather ..

"'Now, as to the other knave. There are trees and to spare, but we have scarce leisure to make for them. Draw they sword, Thomas of Redbridge, and hew me his head from his shoulders.'

"'But, sir,' said Alleyne, who was white to the lips at these bloody doings, 'he hath not yet come to trial.'

"'Young clerk,' said the bailiff, 'you speak of that of which you know nothing. It is true that he hath not come to trial, but the trial hath come to him. He hath fled the law, and is beyond its pale.'

"One of the archers drew his sword and stepped up to the doomed man. The clerk hurried away in horror; but, ere he had gone many paces, he heard a sudden sullen thump, with a choking whistling sound at the end of it. A minute later the bailiff and four of his men rode past him on their journey back to Southampton, the other two having been chosen as grave diggers. As they passed, Alleyne saw that one of the men was wiping his sword blade upon the mane of his horse.

"A deadly sickness came over Alleyne at the sight and, sitting down by the wayside he burst out aweeping, with his nerves all a jangle. It was a terrible world, thought he, and it was hard to know which were the more to be dreaded, the knaves or the men of the law."

The first is a picture taken from the year 1194 A.D. The second describes the fate of outlaws captured in 1366 A.D. Somewhere between these two pictures was, doubtless, the real life of the outlaw. "He was the ancestor of the convict" says one writer, "and the wilderness was the first penal colony." The population of England in the times described was nearer two millions than three millions. How many of these lived the life of the outlaw can never be known, nor even vaguely estimated. We do know that for one man who was hanged, a score escaped to the wild forests and moors of England, and became masterless men—homicides escaping from blood revenge; thieves and robbers; affrighted serfs who could not pay fines or sought to escape their masters' cruelty; men driven by the harshness of the law to place themselves outside the law; men who had forfeited all, save life itself.

"The justices in eyre who visited Gloucester in 1221 listened to an appaling tale of crime which comprised some 330 acts of homicide. The result of their visitation was that one man was mutilated, and about 14 men were hanged, but about 100 orders for outlawry were given. The period of which they took note was long, and comprised a time of civil war, but even in quiet times few out of many criminals came to their appointed end. In 1256 the Justices in Northumberland heard of 77 murders; four murderers were hanged, 72 were outlawed. They heard of 78 other felonies, for which 14 people were hanged and 54 were outlawed. In 1279, their successors in the same county received reports of 68 cases of murder, which resulted in the hanging of two murderers, and the outlawry of 65, while for 110 burglaries and so forth, 20 malefactors went to the gallows, and 75 were left lawless, but at large."

(Pollock & Maitland, "History of English Law")

If, as Hollinghead states, there were 1900 executions of thieves and vagabonds alone each year in the reign of Henry the Eighth, excluding murderers, and, if we assume that somewhere near the same number of executions took place in earlier reigns, how many fled the Courts and took refuge in outlawry? The outlaw's chief enemy was the sheriff, and the sheriff could not follow him if he escaped into the neighbouring county. Sometimes the Lord, stung by repeated depredations by a neighbouring band, would muster his retainers and attempt to exterminate them, but, if the band were numerous and well led, the attempt was a perilous one. Even the King himself, Edward II., was stopped and robbed near Norwich by one such band, led by Sir Gosseline Denville. This bandit was ultimately run to earth and surrounded by the Sheriff of Yorkshire and 500 men, but although the posse had the advantage of a surprise attack, the fight put up by Denville and his followers was so formidable that 200 men were killed before he, and his brother, were captured.

Outlawry, in very early days, was, in all probability not a legal sentence, but a consequence of the flight of the criminal, or alleged criminal. Every man's hand was against him; he was outside the law, a "wolf's head," to be killed where found; he was a public enemy. "A man who refused to do justice to others according to the law, could only be put out of the protection of the law, except in the cases which were grave enough to call for a special expedition against him." The phrase "outlaw against all the people" found in Anglo-Saxon laws, proves that outlawry was known to the law of those times. In early Norman times the hundred-courts had acquired the power to pronounce legal sentences of outlawry on non-appearance before the Court, and such pronouncements have continued to be the basis of the law of outlawry down to modern times. Very early the idea developed of calling the accused at three successive Courts, followed by sentence of outlawry if the offender failed to appear. In the thirteenth century, his appearance had to be demanded at five Courts, and, as this would have caused interminable delay if these five Courts had been ordinary Courts, it is thought that special Courts, by adjournment, were held to meet this difficulty and to shorten the time after which the sentence could be pronounced.

In Anglo-Saxon times, too, the outlaw was a "Friendlessman," because he forfeited his friends; for if any rendered him assistance they were liable to the same punishment. So far as civil rights were concerned he was deemed dead; he could not sue in any Court, nor had he any legal rights which could be enforced, but he, himself, was personally liable upon all causes of action.

The early law was that he could be killed by anyone, anywhere, but by the thirteenth century this seems to have been modified and he could only be killed if he defended himself, or ran away. Once taken, his life was in the King's hands, and anyone killing him had to answer for it as for any other homicide.

Whilst at large the King was entitled to lay waste his land for a year and a day (that strange period which also applied to deodands, and still applies to manslaughter) and then it escheated to the lord. The King could "in-law" him. But the in-lawed person was not the old person restored to legal life; he was a new person! He might recover his lands, but his chattels were irretrievably lost.

So far-reaching were the consequences of outlawry that even his blood was held to be tainted, and the child born to him after the felony was incapable of inheriting, not only from him, but from anyone else.

His life was a hard one. Doubtless, when he joined himself to a band of the "law-less" and "friendless" men, life would not be one constant flight. The band must have acquired some more or less permanent dwelling place in huts, or caves; their wives would come to them; children would be born in the wilderness; and life again assume something of a settled aspect. But the danger was always lurking near; there were hard times in winter; and, when constant depredation and foray had made a district at last too unsafe to stay, the band must move on, and start afresh. There was constant fighting, too, and the wounds and sickness to be faced, and always the possibility of the last desperate fight for life, ending, if unsuccessful, in the hangman's rope, and the gibbet. Women were not oulawed. So dependent was the woman deemed to be upon the man, so subordinate to him, that the law was thus far contemptuous of her, but, if she joined her husband, or her lover, there was the hardship, the discomfort, and the perpetual fear, and when her man had at last been killed, she was indeed outcast.

Outlawry involved not only those consequences already touched upon, but it lost to the accused, if captured, the right of trial. he could be sent to the gallows as soon as the mere fact of outlawry was proved, without regard to his guilt or innocence upon the original charge. In 1234 A.D. this practice received a check when Hubert de Burgh, who had been outlawed, having neither been indicted, nor having appealed, obtained a declaration that his outlawry was null and void upon those grounds, although he had broken prison, and the King was treating him as a rebel.

There is a statute of Henry VI. which extended the process of outlawry to rioters and other offenders (1452-4) under which the usual procedure was somewhat varied and, instead of the customary calling at five successive Courts, the Chancellor was ordered to issue writs to appear within a month, these to be executed by the Sheriff (on pain of a fine of £200). There is a curious distinction, too, in the penalties laid down, for although a lord was liable, on non-appearance, to forfeit office, fees, possessions and estates, and other persons having estates also suffered forfeiture of them, outlawry was reserved only for the person who had no estates.

The many statutes of "praemunire" laid down certain penalties which amounted, in effect, to forfeiture and outlawry. Originally framed to curb the power of the Popes to levy taxes in England, and to control the gifts of benefices, and, further, to prevent appeals to foreign ecclesiastical Courts, the long series of Acts, beginning in 1306 and continuing down to the reign of George III., ultimately covered many offences, the punishment for which placed the offender outside the King's protection, and led to the forfeiture to the Crown of his lands and tenements, goods and chattels. The word "Praemunire" literally means "forewarned."

A person charged under these statutes was not entitled to claim trial by his peers; he was liable to be tried by a jury.

Amongst the many offences to which the statutes of praemunire could be applied were matters so diverse as: molesting the possessors of abbey-lands granted by Parliament to Henry VIII. and Edward VI.; attempting to restrain the importation of gunpowder (16 Car: I. c.21); asserting maliciously and advisedly, by speaking or writing, that both or either of the Houses of Parliament had a legislative authority without sovereign (13. Car: 2 c.1) knowingly or wilfully solemnizing, assisting or being present at forbidden marriages of such descendents of George II. as were prohibited from marrying without the consent of the Crown.

There was a curious threat of outlawry by the West Riding Quarter Sessions, in their proceedings of April 2nd, 1611 (James I.) directed against a whole class of people—the alehouses keepers of Skipton in Yorkshire. What their offence had been is not stated. An "exigent" (a writ, directed to the sheriff to proclaim and call the defendant five County Court days, one after the other, requiring him to appear on pain of outlawry) had been previously issued, but, apparently, some extenuating circumstances had transpired in the meantime, so that it was "Ordered, that a supersedias" (a stay of proceedings) "shall be awarded ye Sheriff to stay ye exigent against ye alehouse-keepers of Scipton, and in regard many of them are poore, and unable to pay due fees, therefore it is ordered that neither the clarke of the peace, nor the clarke of the county, shall take above 2s. 6d. for making and allowing of ye same supersedias."

In the great persecution of the Quakers, following the return to the throne of the evil Stuarts, every method of persecution was used against those defenceless and law-abiding people, including outlawry.

An Act of 1605, which had been passed for the persecution of the Roman Catholics in the time of James I., was revived. Under the Act, anyone refusing to take the oath of allegiance might be outlawed, and imprisoned with the loss of all his goods. This, which was called a sentence of "Praemunire," was passed against a great many Friends.

In 1658, Judge Fell, of Swarthmore, near Ulverstone, died. He had been one of His Majesty's Justices of Assize, and also Vice-Chancellor of the Duchy of Lancaster, Chancellor of the Duchy Court of Westminster, and a Justice, and for some years was a member of Parliament for Lancaster. George Fox was a constant visitor to his home, and, after his death he married Judge Fell's widow, Margaret Fell.

Under the Act of 1605, she was commanded to take the oath of allegience, and, upon her refusal (owing to her religious objection to oaths only) she was committed to Lancaster Castle to await trial at the next Assizes. She was warned at the trial that the penalty for refusal would be forfeiture of all her property and imprisonment for life. She would only reply, "I must keep my conscience clear, however I may suffer," and so was led back again to the gloomy Castle prison.

Three times she was brought to the bar, and her lawyers pleaded for her, but all in vain. On July 21st, 1664, Judge Turner passed sentence of "Praemunire" against her, by which she was outlawed, condemned to imprisonment for life, and all her property forfeited to the Crown. Her courageous reply was, "Although I am out of the King's protection, I am not out of the protection of the Almighty God."

She was in gaol for four and a half years, but, although there were frequent threats later in her life to enforce the confiscation of her property, this was never actually carried out.

Out of the 12,000 Friends who suffered imprisonment between 1661 and 1689 (300 of whom died in prison) many actually suffered the full penalties of outlawry and forfeiture of their possessions.

Outlawry in civil proceedings was abolished by statute in 1879 and the outlaw once more became competent to sue in these Courts, but it remained a possible weapon of the law in criminal proceedings against accused persons who failed to surrender to their bail, and to take their trial, until January 1st, 1939, the date on which the Administration of Justice (Miscellaneous Provisions) Act, 1938, came into force. In five words "Outlawry proceedings . . . . are hereby abolished," (Section 12), that Act brought to an end the power of the State to place outside its protection those who feared to face their trial for their alleged crimes. The fourth schedule to the Act contains a long list of old statutes which by the abolition of outlawry, cease to be law, but remain history.

In Scotland, outlawry still lingers, and a case in a Scottish Court, so recently as March, 1939, reminds Scotsmen that failure to answer to bail, and to stand their trial, for an indictable offence, still subjects them to forfeiture of chattels, to loss of estates, and to the withdrawal of the protection of their country.

In America, too, so recently as November, 1938, four persons were each sentenced to two years in the penitentiary for conspiring to harbour an outlaw (three of them being ex-policemen). How the person who was the subject of the conspiracy became an outlaw - whether by the pronouncement of a Court of Law; as a result of some picturesque but inaccurate journalistic description; or merely because his crimes had placed him outside the pale,—was not stated.

CHAPTER V.

THE ORDEAL

The ordeal has been used in countries all over the world from the beginning of history, and before. In principle it has always followed certain recognised lines which involved an appeal to the Almighty for a miraculous decision as to the truth of an accusation. In some of the less civilised countries it is still carried out, generally under the control of the priests, but it has long since disappeared from amongst the more civilised peoples.

A very early use of the ordeal is recorded in the fifth chapter of Numbers, which describes the mode of administering to a woman accused of unfaithfulness, bitter water mixed with dust from the tabernacle floor, with a curse laid upon her if she were guilty.

In Saxon days it was frequently used in England. One well-known form was the ordeal of walking barefoot over glowing ploughshares, generally nine in number. If the accused person succeeded in passing through them, or if he trod upon any and received no harm, he was declared by the Judge to be innocent. Emma, mother of Edward the Confessor (1044-1066 A.D.) and great-aunt of William the Conqueror, underwent this form of the ordeal upon an accusation that she had been too friendly with the Bishop of Winchester. "Being blindfolded unto the place where the glowing hot irons were laid, she went forward with her bare feet, and so passed over them, and being gone over them all, and not knowing whether she were past them or not, said, 'O, Good Lord! when shall I come to the place of my purgation? And having her eyes uncovered, and seeing herself to have passed over them, she kneeled down and gave thanks to God for manifesting her innocence by her preservation from being hurt."

An interesting story, even though it may leave the critical reader still unconvinced as to the good lady's innocence!

In the Saxon criminal law the ordeal took any one of four forms. These were (1) the camp-fight or combat; (2) The fire ordeal; (3) The hot water ordeal; and (4) The cold water ordeal. The ordeal of the hot ploughshares, which Emma underwent, was one form of the fire ordeal.

THE CAMP-FIGHT OR COMBAT

The camp-fight (or the combat, to give it its more familiar name) was in effect the duel, fought between two champions. The accused might choose another to fight in his stead, but the accuser was bound to take up arms himself to support his accusation, and there was to be equality of weapons. If the crime alleged against the accused was one deserving death, the combat was for life or death, so that, if the accused's champion was defeated the accused was adjudged guilty and suffered execution. If the offence carried only imprisonment, the fight was over when one had subdued the other, so as to make him yield himself prisoner. Priests and women were allowed a champion to represent them.

Sir Walter Scott has drawn a vivid picture of the trial by combat in his "Ivanhoe" - Rebecca, the Jewess, accused of sorcery before the Grand Master of the Temple, making her appeal:-

"'There is yet one chance of life left to me, even by your own fierce laws .. .. I deny this charge; I maintain my innocence, and I declare the falsehood of this accusation—I challenge the privilege of trial by combat, and will appear by my champion.'"

This was followed by the fight in the lists between Wilfred, her champion, and the Templar Brian de Bois Guilbert.

The Templar dies at the moment of the impact in the lists, and Wilfred demands of the Grand Master, as Judge of the field, if he had manfully, and rightfully, done his duty in the combat.

"'Manfully and rightfully hath it been done,' said the Grand Master, 'I pronounce the maiden free and guiltless—the arms and body of the deceased knight are at the will of the victor.'"

The earlier Saxon trial by combat was, in all probability, a much simpler matter than the elaborate spectacle which it became under the Norman rule, and it is likely that it took the form of a single combat, on foot, at the shire moot, at some suitable spot adjacent to, or in, the camp of the Saxons, which would be temporarily established while the Court was sitting.

Shakespeare has admirably depicted the Norman trial by combat in the opening scene of "Richard II.," where Henry Bolingbroke, Duke of Hereford, challenges Thomas Duke of Norfolk, and there is a further description of trial by combat by Sir Walter Scott in "The Fair Maid of Perth."

In later Norman times, men in high positions ran a considerable risk of receiving a challenge to combat from their critics, as in the case of Henry of Essex, hereditary standard bearer to the King, who, in one of Henry II.'s punitive expeditions against the Welsh, threw down his standard and bolted from the field. Accused of felony by Robert de Montfort, and challenged to single combat, the unfortunate Essex was not only vanquished in the lists, but his estates were forfeited, and he himself thrust into a monastery.

One of the later instances occured in England, in the reign of Elizabeth (1571) when the lists were actually prepared for the combat, and the Judges of the Common Pleas appeared at Tothill Field as umpires of the combat. Fortunately, or unfortunately, the petitioner failed to put in an appearance, and was consequently non-suited.

Actually, the last claim to a trial by battle was raised so late as 1817 in the case of Thornton v. Ashford, when Lord Ellenborough found himself obliged to give the ruling that "The general law of the land is that there shall be a trial by battle in cases of appeal unless the party brings himself within some of the exceptions." Thornton was accused of murdering Mary Ashford, and claimed his right to challenge the appellant, the brother of the murdered girl, to wager of battle. His suit was allowed, and, the challenge being refused, the accused escaped.

But the attention of the Government having been drawn to the fact that this barbaric type of trial had not been abolished, the law was abolished the following year by 59, Geo. III., c.46.

THE FIRE ORDEAL

The ordeal by fire, used in accusations in which there was no manifest proof, denied by the accused, was another of the Saxon ordeals, later used by the Normans. In addition to the ordeal of the ploughshares, previously referred to, the accused could be adjudged to take a red-hot iron, and to hold it in his bare hand. After prayers and invocations, the accused was bound to accept this ordeal, or, in default, to be found guilty of the crime of which he was accused, and was punished according to law.

The Bedouin may still be ordered to undergo this ordeal, but he has to lick the white-hot iron. It seems to be conceded that, if the metal is white hot, and clean, the ordeal may be carried through without harm to the accused, and H. V. Morton, in his book, "In the Steps of the Master," tells a very striking story of a trial at Beersheba, at which he was present, in which a suitor to the Court demanded the trial by fire.

"'He is demanding the trial by fire,' said Arif el Arif, 'I do not think we shall allow it in this case.'

"'You don't mean to say that you permit trial by fire?'

"'It is the most respected verdict of all. The whole desert respects the trial by fire,' he replied. 'The men who administer it are known as 'Mobishaa,' and the ordeal itself is 'Bishaa.' there are only two such men in all Arabia, one in Sinai, and one in the Hedjaz. We employ the man from Sinai.

"The method is this. The 'Mobishaa' first asks for a confession. If this is not made, he takes fire and heats an iron until it is white hot, and covered with white sparks. He then collects his fee! This is £10. Defendant and plaintiff each give him £5, and at the end of the ordeal he returns half the fee to the innocent party.

"The accused steps forward, is given water to wash out his mouth, and is then asked to lick the red hot iron three times. At the end of this ordeal the 'Mobishaa' examines his tongue and gives judgement. It is an extraordinary thing—and you will think I am romancing—but I have seen men pass unscathed through the ordeal.

"'But that can have nothing to do with their guilt or innocence,' I said.

"'On the contrary, I believe it has. The guilty man is so terrified that his mouth goes dry, and he gets terribly burned. But the innocent man's saliva continues to flow, and he does not show anything on his tongue after the ordeal but a redness. Anyhow, the 'Mobishaa's' verdict is never questioned. It is the verdict of Allah!'"

The Saxons gave a little more lattitude to the man who went through this terrific ordeal, and he was held to be not guilty if his hand, though burned,

BOUNDARY STONE NEAR BISHOP BURTON

THE SANCTUARY KNOCKER, DURHAM CATHEDRAL

NORTH DOOR, BEVERLEY MINSTER
(The porter's room is above the door)

healed within a given time (three days is the period mentioned by some writers).

THE HOT WATER ORDEAL

In this type of ordeal boiling hot water was used, the suspected person being ordered by the Judge to put his arms up to the elbows in the water. Sometimes boiling oil was used instead of boiling water.

THE COLD WATER ORDEAL

This trial was "ordinarily used for the common sort of people, who, having a cord tied about them under their arms, were cast into some river, and if they sank to the bottom until they were drawn up, which was in a very short limited space, then were they held guiltless; but such as did remain upon the water were held culpable, being, as they said, of the water rejected and kept up."

The directions given by a German Archbishop in the ninth century provided that the accused must be fastened by a rope, that he might not be in danger if the water received him as innocent, but might be pulled out.

In the later Middle Ages this ordeal by "swimmimg" became the approved method of trying a suspected witch. The right thumb was bound to the left toe, and the left thumb to the right toe, and, in this hapless state she was thrown into the pond or river, in which, if she was guilty, it was thought impossible for her to sink. The distressing cases which occured in England in later years in which the suspected witches were "ducked," were a survival of this cruel superstition that their guilt could be proved by this means.

The persecution of witches was ended by the statute 9 Geo: 11, c.5 (1736).

It is possible that the use of the ducking-stool for women was, originally, a development of the ordeal by cold water.

The water ordeal, though successfully faced by the accused, did not always lead to his acquittal. Henry II. ordained that, in cases of murder or serious felonies, in which the accusation was made by "the legal knights of the county," the man should, even though acquitted by the ordeal, be obliged to leave the realm.

All forms of ordeal were abolished in 1215, by an order of the Roman Catholic Church, but, as has been already said, the trial by combat continued long after that time.

One result of the abolition of trial by fire or water was the development of the jury of presentment in its stead, a jury of 12 knights of the shire, and four witnesses from the place where the alleged crime had been committed. This development, in due time, led to the creation of the Grand Jury, and the petty jury of our own times.

CHAPTER VI.

BENEFIT OF CLERGY

Benefit of Clergy was not a punishment—it was a privilege which operated to prevent punishment by the criminal Courts—but it played such an important part in the history of the law of England for some centuries that it is necessary to devote a brief chapter to its consideration.

William the Conqueror, for the purposes of this hurried review, may be assumed to have been the cause of all the trouble. When he had dealt with the unwilling Saxons and had effectively persuaded them to submit to the Norman rule, and had time to turn his attention to the administration of the law, he found that, in the shire-moot or County Court, it was the practice for the bishop to sit with the ealdorman, the two acting as Judges. William owed a great deal to the Church, and, probably having this in mind, he removed the bishop from the shire-moot, and gave him a court of his own. From that time, ecclesiastical cases were tried by the bishop, with the assistance later of the archdeacon and other Church dignitaries.

The question now arose whether clergymen who were accused of crime were to be tried by the bishop, or by the ordinary criminal Court, the shire-moot. The point was an important one, for the Bishop's Court could not inflict a sentence of death, but only a fine, or imprisonment in a monastery or deprive a man of his clerical orders. As, in those days, there were no less than seven orders of clergy, so that, practically, every educated man who was not a soldier was included in the numbers of clergy, the real point of the dispute was whether educated persons were to be punished, when they committed crime, with less severity than if they were ignorant.

The difficulty had not been settled in 1067, when the Conqueror ended his life in France, nor was it really faced during the next three reigns (William Rufus, Henry I., and Stephen), and when Henry II. came to the throne in 1154, he and his friend, Thomas a Becket, were fully occupied for some years in dealing with the confusion and anarchy in the country caused by Stephen's incompetence. When the barons had been curbed and their castles destroyed; the debased coinage restored; and the Scots and the french taught a lesson, Henry had time to turn to the country's administration, and almost immediately he and Becket (now Archbishop of Canterbury) came to a deadlock as to the trial of the clergy.

Henry urged that if a clergyman committed a murder or other serious crime, he should be handed over to the criminal court for trial; Becket appears to have contended that, if a clergyman committed such a crime, it would be sufficient to unfrock him, so that, if he committed a second crime, he would be a layman, and could be hanged as such. In other words, Becket's contention appears to have been that it should take two murders to hang a clergyman, but one only to hang a layman, while the King demanded that a clergyman, tried, convicted and unfrocked by the Ecclesiastical Court, should be handed back to the Sheriff to be hanged or otherwise. Apparently a case had just occured in which the offender had been gravely under-punished by the Ecclesiastical Court, so that the question had become an immediate one.

The tragic sequel is well-known to us from our history books—the King's anger; the four knights and their murderous visit to Canterbury; the death of Becket in the Cathedral. Unfortunately, the death of Becket so weakened the King's cause that we have the melancholy story of his abject pilgrimage to the tomb of the murdered Archbishop, followed by a loss of prestige, and the strengthening of the case for the Church. The result which actually followed was that clergy went unpunished, or were only lightly punished, and that the Church established its claim—one which led in the course of hundreds of years to frightful injustices and evils—to exemption from trial by the ordinary Courts; in other words, the Church secured the right to that privilege which has ever since been known by the name of "Benefit of Clergy." In effect, the Church secured exemption to everyone who could shew the slightest official association with the ecclesiastical organisation, from punishment of death. The unreasonable temper of the King and the great Churchman, and the swords of the four murderers, deprived England of many important rights which were recovered only at the time of the Reformation, and history shews only too clearly that benefit of clergy became one of the worst evils of the Middle Ages, and later.

"Not only monks and parish priests, but professional men and an enormous crowd of menials and minor officers of the clerical establishments, and in later times, *anyone who could make some show of being able to read,* were safe from the dread of any serious penalty for such crimes as burglary, rape, and homicide, at any rate for the first offence. It was only too easy to obtain minor orders in the Church, and the attraction to baser spirits of such privileges and protections were great."

(G.M. Trevelyan, "History of England.")

By the time Henry VIII. came to the throne the number of those who could claim benefit of clergy had become incalculable, for, in addition to those attached to Cathedrals, the Churches and the Universities, there were no less than 600 monastic houses where dwelt men and women devoted to the service of the Church. To such orders as the Benedictine, the Clugniac, the Cistercian, the Augustinian and a multitude of other religious houses, there were to be added the military orders—the Templars, and the Knights of St. John, or Hospitaliers—and the mendicant (begging) friars who had houses in every town, such as the White Friars, the Grey Friars, and the Black Friars, the whole comprising an army of many hundreds of thousands, and this at a time when the population of the whole of England was under five millions.

The only women who could claim Benefit of Clergy were the nuns, for the reason that no women could be Church officials, and when the Reformation broke up the nunneries, women were, for a time, left without the privilege, but a compromise was effected whereby women who were married were included, and in 1692 women were again allowed to claim Benefit of Clergy.

It has already been recorded that, ultimately anyone able to read could be included in the great privileged class. It should be remembered that the test of ability to read rested on no more than the ability to read one verse of a psalm, verse one of the 51st psalm:-

"Have mercy upon me, O god, according to thy loving-kindness; according unto the multitude of thy tender mercies, blot out my transgressions."

Anyone who could memorise this brief verse was immune from the death penalty. The verse was known as the "neck-verse," presumably because the correct recital of the verse saved the culprit's neck from the executioner. In 1705, even this very slight test was abolished.

The state endeavoured to counter the constant increase in those who were escaping the death penalty, by removing, from time to time, the more serious offences from Benefit of Clergy, and with some success. Henry II. had already excluded the many offences under the Forest Laws, and by Edward I's reign (1272) those minor offences which later became the misdemeanours of the present penal code, were excluded. Edward III. excluded treason, and Henry VIII. removed a large number of offences from Benefit of Clergy.

In the meantime, in 1487, it had been enacted that every layman convicted of a clergyable felony should be branded on the thumb. This was an effective way of recording that he had had this one immunity, and of ensuring that he did not, by an oversight, secure his Benefit of Clergy a second time.

By the end of the seventeenth century a conviction for any of the following crimes meant a death sentence for anyone, clergyman or laymen, without exception: High and petty treason, piracy, murder, arson, burglary, housebreaking and putting in fear, highway robbery, horse stealing, stealing from a person of the value of 12d. and all robberies. From this point as statute after statute was passed, it was laid down that the punishment should be "without benefit of clergy."

But, as Albert Lieck, in his delightful book, "Justice and Police in England" says, "Becket's blood remains splashed on the pages of our statute-book even to the present time. The special forms of theft made non-clergyable were, when the punishment of death for them was taken away, still provided for by specially heavy punishments. When the law of larceny was consolidated in 1916, these absurd distinctions, though they have no relation to the degree of guilt of the accused, were retained . . . Thus, even to-day, Thomas a Becket's ghost stands in every police court, sternly forbidding the magistrates to try a man for stealing a horse . . . Nothing better illustrates the continuity of English history, and how peculiarly illogical is the English mind, than this strange tangle between capital punishment and the privilege of the Churchman."

Two points only in conclusion. It is an interesting fact that, stoutly as the Church held to the privilege it had so nearly lost at the time of the murder of Thomas a Becket, there were certain offences which, in view of its own limited powers of punishment, it was willing to hand over to the criminal courts so as to secure the death of the criminal, but these were offences which the Church regarded as offences not so much against the State as against itself and its creeds. They were heresy, apostacy, and sorcery, and the penalty in these cases was death by burning.

The second point is that in spite of the evils of Benefit of Clergy, the Church's ideal throughout the centuries was higher than that of the State, and that it did protect from death countless thousands who in those days of savage laws, would otherwise have been put to death for trifling and unimportant offences, and many thousands more would, but for its protection, have fallen victims to the intolerance and persecution of kings and nobles. The Church stood, too, for culture and knowledge, for healing and sanitation, and, perhaps most important of all, it organised and maintained a great system of poor relief, which often stood between the poor of all ages and death by starvation.

Benefit of Clergy was abolished by an Act of 1827, but as the statute did not repeal a statute of 1547 (under which peers were given the privilege) a further statute had to be passed in 1841, putting peers on the same footing as commons and clergy.

CHAPTER VII.

SANCTUARY

For over a thousand years there were in England sacred places which afforded refuge, protection, and the right of asylum. Sanctuary is mentioned in the laws of the Saxons; it was widely used under the Norman kings. The general right of sanctuary protected only those guilty of felonies, and applied to every church in the country. Peculiar sanctuary derived its power from the charter given by the King, and gave immunity even to those accused of high or petty treason, not for a specified time only, but apparently for life. Of these chartered sanctuaries there appear to have been about 22, the list including such famous churches as Beaulieu, Beverley, Durham, Lancaster, Ripon, Westminster, Winchester and York.

Every church in England, therefore, represented the jealously-guarded right of the church to intervene between the criminal and the State, and, upon certain terms, to protect him from the death penalty.

It is true that sanctuary was not limited only to the criminal, for it offered the poor and wronged asylum and protection against their oppressors, and one who had unwittingly committed that which was regarded as a crime by the law of the land might save himself from a criminal's death. In some cases the pursued must get his hand upon the knocker of the door before he was safe; in others he found sanctuary in some prescribed part of the building, or in the sanctuary chair; in the case of the great churches the fugitive, on passing the outermost sanctuary post or cross, perhaps a mile away from the church, had reached safety from the hue and cry and the Sheriff's posse; from his pursuing lord, or the avenger of his victim.

Other rights of sanctuary included the prescriptive right of sanctuary attaching to the King's palaces. In Anglo-Saxon times this extended to the palace and 3,000 paces around it. It extended to the King himself beyond the precincts. At the present time members of Parliament have certain rights within the precincts of the Houses of Parliament. During the Irish agitations of the 'eighties of the last century, Irish members actually avoided arrest by living in the House, and never passing outside the gates of the palace yard. The houses of ambassadors were in the past, and possibly may be in the present, limited sanctuaries.

'The best, and as a rule, the only practicable chance of escape open to the pursued lay in the possibility of his reaching a sanctuary before the hunters came up with him. If a man took sanctuary his life was safe, but he remained a close prisoner within the precincts of the asylum in which he had found refuge until he received the King's pardon, or until he had purchased his freedom by 'abjuring the realm,' an undertaking which entailed upon him perpetual banishment, and the forfeiture of all his belongings.

"These sacred asylums within which the law was powerless, were often made use of in a manner never contemplated when the privilege affording protection to fugitives was first extended to them.

"If an offender was very unpopular his chance of reaching sanctuary was very remote. It was easy to head him off or to surround the place in such a manner that approach meant certain capture. On the other hand, if the country folk were disposed to favour the escape of the hunted man, there was little difficulty in managing the pursuit so that he should reach his goal in safety."

(Melville Lee in "History of Police in England")

The above statement that "it was easy to head the fugitive off or to surround the place" needs some qualification, for the murderer or the robber did not, necessarily, head for the nearest sanctuary. Some sanctuaries were more popular than others, and occasionally an offender from, say, Oxford, would head north for Beverley, rather than turn south for Winchester or Beaulieu.

The list of those who sought sanctuary at Beverley, for instance, proves that fugitives came there from all over England, and in many cases left other sanctuaries behind them in their own towns—Oxford, Salisbury, Ripon, Durham, London, Lichfield. and from far afield, men headed for the security of Beverley—from Westmorland and Pembroke; from Ipswich and Carlisle; from Shrewsbury and from Bridgewater, for the sanctuary of St. John of Beverley was under the direct protection of the Archbishop of York, who ruled the town, and maintained his rights with an iron discipline.

There were cases in which it was not wise to rush to the nearest sanctuary; local hatreds, though very rarely, proved stronger than even the fear of the consequences, and sanctuary was, at times, violated.

There were several breaches of sanctuary in the reign of Richard the Lionheart, but in two cases the breach brought down in disgrace the justiciars who virtually ruled England during the prolonged absence of the King.

Geoffrey, Archbishop of York, returned to England contrary to his promise to stay away, and was arrested at Dover and dragged from the sanctuary by the partisans of William Longchamps. The justiciar, alarmed at the tumult caused by this sacrilege, refused to meet the Council and took refuge in London, but he was deposed. In 1198, Hubert Walter, Archbishop of Canterbury, and justiciar, allowed the arrest of William FitzOsbert, a dangerous agitator, who had taken sanctuary. The Church of St. Mary-le-Bowe was fired over the man, and he was dragged out and executed at Tyburn. Again the Church was too strong for the powerful minister, and he was compelled to surrender his office.

A third case, in 1232 (Henry III.) also concerned a justiciar of England, Hubert de Burgh, but he was the victim, and not the perpetrator of the outrage. He was dragged from sanctuary (a chapel at Brantwood), and a smith was ordered to shackle him. The smith was a bold man, "I will die any death," he replied, "before I put iron on the man who freed England from the stranger and saved Dover from France." On remonstrances of the Bishop of London, de Burgh was replaced in sanctuary, but hunger compelled him to surrender, and he was imprisoned in the Tower.

Henry VIII., in a brief statute of 1529 (an Act which remained on the statute-book until the reign of James I.) laid down a procedure in cases of felony and murder:-

"An Act concerning such as shall take Sanctuary for Felony or Murder.
"Every person taking Sanctuary for Felony or Murder
"shall take his Abjuration and Passage when required
"by the Crown, and shall be marked with the letter A
"on his Thumb with a hot iron; and if he refuse to
"take his passage at the Time appointed by the Coroner,
"he shall lose the Benefit of Sanctuary."

But this had been the custom long before 1529, and was probably only a re-enactment of previous statutes, with the exception, possibly of the portion relating to branding on the thumb.

When the criminal had made his confession to the Court attached to the sanctaury, and had abjured the realm, he was compelled to make the journey to the seaport mentioned in the order of the Court, without delay, and Sir Arthur Conan Doyle, in his book, "The White Company" (chapter XIV.), has described such a journey.

Sir Nigel and the White Company, marching to Southampton, overtook two men "one a pace behind the other . . . The first was a mishapen, squalid man, with cruel, cunning eyes, and a shock of tangled red hair, bearing in his hands a small unpainted cross, which he held high so that all men might see it . . . Behind him, with his toe rasping ever upon the other's heels, there walked a very stern black-bearded man, with a hard eye and a set mouth. He bore over his shoulder a great knotted stick, with three jagged nails stuck in the head of it, and from time to time he whirled it up in the air as though he could scarce hold back from dashing his companion's brains out. So in silence they walked under the spread of the branches on the grass-grown path from Boldre."

Sir Nigel halted his company and in the course of his conversation with the black-bearded man, he learnt the meaning of this strange scene:—

"'This man is Peter Peterson, a very noted rieve, draw-latch and murderer, who has wrought much evil for many years in the parts about Winchester," said the black-bearded man. 'It was but the other day he slew my younger brother William in Bere Forest, for which—by the black thorn of Glastonbury—I shall have his heart's blood, though I walked behind him to the further end of the earth.'

"'But if this indeed be so,' asked Sir Nigel, 'why is it that you have come with him so far through the forest?'

"Because I am an honest Englishman, and will take no more than the law allows. For when the deed was done, this foul and base wretch fled to sanctuary at St. Cross, and I, as you may think, after him with all the posse.

"'The Prior, however, hath so ordered that while he holds this cross no man may lay any hand upon him without the ban of the Churh, which heaven forfend for me and mine. Yet, if for an instant he lays his cross aside, or if he fail to journey to Pitt's deep, where it is ordered that he shall take ship to outland parts, or if he take not the first ship, or if, until the ship be ready, he walk not every day into the sea so far as his loins, then he becomes outlaw, and I shall forthwith dash out his brains.'

At this the man sitting on the ground snarled up at him like a rat, while the other clenched his teeth and shook his club, and looked down at him with murder in his eyes. Knight and squires looked from rogue to avenger, but as it was a matter upon which none could mend, they tarried no longer and went upon their way. Looking back, they saw that the murderer had drawn bread and cheese from his scrip, and was silently munching it, with the protecting cross still hugged to his breast, while the other, black and grim, stood in the sunlit road, and threw his dark shadow athwart him."

Such were the sights to be seen on the roads to the seaports of England in the year of our Lord 1366.

How far back we have to travel through English history to find the beginning of this strange privilege of sanctuary no one can say, but the law of 693 A. D. definitely says, "If any one accused of a capital offence flies to a Church, his life shall be spared, and he shall make a compensation according to justice. If any one deserving the whip or the scourge takes refuge there, the stripes shall be forgiven him."

Later, Alfred the Great (871-901) laid down that anyone who "shall violate the sanctaury by inflicting upon the fugitive bonds, wounds or blows, shall be bound to pay the price which the law awarded to the injury, and the great sum of 120 shillings to the ministers of the Church."

(Note- "The price which the law awarded "referred to a scale of fines used by the Saxons. For instance, a wound of an inch long, under the hair, fine 1/-. One of a like size on the face, 2/-. The loss of an ear, 30/-, and so forth.)

King Edmund (1016) ordained that no criminal should be killed who sought refuge in the church, or any of the King's towns. The King himself declared that his house should give no protection to murderers until they had satisfied the Church by their penance, and the kindred of the deceased by compensation.

Probably the custom had persisted from the earliest ages, for, 1400 years at least before the time of Christ, Moses set aside three cities of refuge (Deuteronomy IV., 41-43), "That the slayer might flee thither, which should kill his neighbour unawares, and hated him not in time past, and that fleeing unto one of these cities he might live."

Henry VIII. seems to have taken considerable interest in sanctuaries, for, in addition to the Act already mentioned, there were others. An Act of 1530-1 tightened up the law considerably, on very practical grounds, for, after reciting that a great number of men had fled to "Churches, and other hallowed places within the realm," many of whom had subsequently abjured the realm and gone to other countries, it went on to point out that many of these men were expert mariners or men versed in war, who had trained foreign troops in archery, and who had further disclosed State secrets "to the no little damage and prejudice of the realm."

A further Act of 1535-6 ordained that sanctuary persons should wear badges, and should not carry weapons, nor should they go abroad before sunrise, nor after sunset, and that they should not resist their Governors.

But the great conflict with the Church was becoming more embittered, and the measures against its power more severe, and in 1540, Henry, in an Act dealing with sanctuaries, privileges and Churchyards, severely curtailed the number of places recognised as sanctuaries. This important measure ran as follows:-

"All Sanctuaries and Places privileged, which have been used for Sanctuary, shall be utterly extinguished, except Parish Churches and their Churchyards, Cathedral Churches, Hospitals, and Churches Collegiate, and all Churches dedicated, used as Parish Churches and the Sanctuaries to either of them belonging, and Wells in the County of Somerset, Westminster, Manchester, Northampton, Norwich, York, Derby and Lancaster. None of the said Places shall give Immunity or Defence to any Person which shall commit wilful Murder Rape Burglary Robbery in the Highway or in any House, or in any Church or Chapel or which shall burn wilfully any House, or Barn with Corn. He that taketh Sanctuary in any Church Churchyard, etc., may remain there forty days as hath been used unless the Coroner repair to him to take his Abjuration; in which case he shall abjure to any of the aforesaid privileged Places, not being full of the Number appointed to them, viz above twenty Persons, there to remain during Life. If a privileged Person, daily called to appear before the Governor, shall make Default three Days, or if he commit any Felony, he shall lose the Benefit of Sanctuary. A privileged Person abjuring to any of the aforesaid Places, shall be conducted from Constable to Constable directly, until he be brought to the Governor of the said privileged Place; and if that Place be full of his Number, then he shall be conducted to the next privileged Place, and so to the next, etc., until etc.,"

In the following year the privilege of sanctuary was taken from Manchester, and transferred to "West Chester."

The remaining rights of sanctuary lasted, as we have seen until the reign of James I., when they were abolished finally (1623).

The most disreputable "sanctuary" in London for years after sanctuary was abolished by an Act of Parliament of the twentieth year of James I. (1623), was Whitefriars, a district lying between Water Lane (now Whitefriars Street) and the Temple, and Fleet Street and the Thames—called in the rogues' cant of that day "Alsatia." The place swarmed with bankrupt citizens, fraudulent debtors, ruined gamesters, cheats and swindlers, with a plentiful sprinkling of bullies and desperadoes of the worst kind, all leagued to resist any interference with their immunities." Not until 1697 were the privileges of Whitefriars and other dens of the same type abolished by the "Escape from Prison Act." Even after that date abuses lingered, and another Act was passed in 1723 to deal with these evil survivals.

Thus it will be seen, the ancient privilege of sanctuary, based in theory at least, upon the primitive and universal belief that the contagion of holiness should offer refuge to the criminal and the afflicted, came to suffer abuse. Originally under the strictest rules and regulations, these refuges were, in

THE FRITH STOOL, BEVERLEY MINSTER

HALIFAX GIBBET (from "Bygone Punishments")
(By courtesy of the publishers Philip Allan & Co.)

lawless times, of great use as a check to "blood vengeance" and oppression, but in the course of centuries, while the rights of sanctuary were jealously guarded, they became in many cases a menace to law and order.

Often, too, the consequences to the community to which the successful fugitive belonged were distressing. Fines and even more severe punishments were inflicted upon villages and parishes in revenge for the escape of the criminal. In the year 1288 a man stabbed a butcher and took refuge in the Church at Crawley, and abjured the realm. As he had thus succeeded in placing himself outside the scope of the criminal law, the townships of Crawley and Hurst were heavily fined in his stead. Such was the result in those days of a failure to bring an offender to justice.

How strongly the faith in sanctuary was held until long after the year 1623 is illustrated by the case of the Osborns, Ruth and John, a husband and wife accused of witchcraft at Tring, on April 22nd, 1757.

The pair sought sanctuary in the church vestry, and in any ordinary circumstances they would have been safe there, but the crowd, inflamed by that bigotry and cruelty which charges of witchcraft always seemed to arouse, dragged them from the Church.

They were then "tried" for witchcraft in the local pond (their thumbs and toes tied in the approved fashion), a chimney sweep named Thomas Coley assisting by turning then over and over in the water with a stick.

The woman died there and then, and the man shortly afterwards.

Mr. Coley, unfortunately for himself, had taken too prominent a part in the alleged "trial." The sequel was that he took a still more prominent part in a trial for murder before Sir William Lee at Hertford Assizes, four months later, and was conducted to the scene of his former exploit, the pond, under a large escort, and there executed, his body adorning the local gibbet for several years afterwards.

CHAPTER VIII.

A YORKSHIRE SANCTUARY

"I topped the rise beyond Bishop Burton" (says H. V. Morton in "The Call of England"). "Below me in green fields lay the ancient town of Beverley . . .

"There come moments in England when travellers pause in their journey, brought to a full stop of mind and body by a beauty so sudden, so old, so right, and so English that there is nothing for a man to do but to look gratefully before him . . . .

"There are certain moments when a man should not be ashamed to fall on his knees by the roadside; and what a strange thought about Beverley! This hilltop must have been the spot on which the pilgrims to the shrine of St. John of Beverley sank down in the meadow-sweet to give thanks for the journey's end.

"At this point fugitives with the blood of a murder still on them took new heart as they raced for sanctuary. There is something strange about these sanctuaries. I noticed it at King's Beaulieu in the New Forest; I notice it at Beverley."

On this very Bishop Burton Road there stands, by the roadside, a broken pillar, believed to be one of those pillars which marked, on the main roads leading into Beverley, long centuries ago, the outer boundary of that sanctuary which the thief, or the murderer, or the fugitive from his enemy, had strained every nerve to reach, for within it lay safety, the sanctuary given by the all-powerful Church of that day.

Within these stones, too, the jurisdiction of the Archbishop was absolute—the Judges of the King could only enter the town by special permit and request, which he could give or with-hold, without appeal. The town of Beverley lay under the firm rule of the Church, through the Archbishop: for good or ill his decision was final.

At Beverley Minster the central point of security was the Frithstool, or Chair of Peace, upon which the criminal sat, and so became absolutely safe. Not even the King's might could seize and bring him forth from that chair. According to old writers the following inscription was carved upon it: -
"This stone seat is called 'Freedstoll,' which means the chair of peace, on reaching which a fugitive criminal hath complete safety."

It is a plain massive chair, so simple in design that its age seems greater than the Minster itself: most likely it dates back at least to the days of the Saxon King, Athelstan.

It was the seventh point of safety. The sixth was the immediate area of the high altar; the fifth commenced at the entrance to the choir; the fourth began at the Church door; the third at the outer gate of the Minster; the second at certain carved crosses in the town; and the first at the stone crosses such as the one in Bishop Burton Road.

Outside that first stone a fugitive was liable to immediate arrest and retribution, without appeal, but within that first stone he was under the protection of the Church. The six boundaries outside the chair were to determine the punishment to be meted out to the pursuer, even the King's Sheriff, who was bold enough to seize the fugitive once he had reached sanctuary. By progressive fines the penalties became greater up to the choir, but he who dared to take a malefactor or a debtor from within the sixth enclosure should be Bote-less (bootless, or beyond help) and his offence such that no money payment could redeem his daring, or his life.

Having gained sanctuary, the fugitive from justice had to take an oath. The details with regard to this oath have been preserved, and were as follows:—

"Procedure of person seeking Sanctuary at Beverley. (Harl. 4292 MS.)

"The Bailiff shall receive the prayer of him seeking the liberty of S. John at Beverley.

"The Clerk of (the Chapter or) the Church shall then write and describe his name in the book of the Church, enquiring as under:-

What man he killed, and wherewith, and both their names, and then order him to lay his hand upon the Book, saying on this wise:—

"'Sir, Take heed on your oath

"'Ye shall be true and faithful to my Lord Archbishop of York, Lord of this Town, to the Provost of the same, to the Canons of this Church, and all other ministers thereof.

"'Also ye shall bear good heart to the Bailiff and the XII. governors of this town, to all burgesses and commoners of the same.

"'Also ye shall bear no pointed weapon, dagger, knife nor none other weapon, against the King's peace.

"'Also ye shall be ready with all your power, if there be any debate or strife, or any sudden case of fire within the town, to help to surcess it.

"'Also ye shall be ready at the obit of King Athelstan at the dirige, and the Mass, at such time as it is done, at the warning of the Bellman of the Town, and do your duty in ringing, and for to offer at the Mass on the morn.

"'So help you God and these holy Evangelists.'

"And then order him to kiss the Book.

"And thus the Bailiff or his deputy shall receive from each seeking the aforesaid liberty, a fee, viz., 2s. 4d. and the Clerk to the Court or his deputy shall receive."

(Note- The fact that those received into sanctuary were expected to actively assist in fire-fighting is borne out by records of the Corporation of the purchase of crooks, with chains, and long poles with hooks on the end, which were to be kept at the Church door for use in the immediate neighbourhood. These were for pulling down the burning thatch from the houses.)

The offenders were treated with kindness, and during the thirty days' grace they had their food provided in the refectory, and, if they were persons of distinction, they were lodged in a dormitory or in a house within the Minster precincts. At the end of the time their privilege protected them to the borders of the county, and they could claim the same security a second time under like circumstances. If, however, anyone's life was saved a third time by the privilege of sanctuary he became permanently a servant of the Church.

As a general rule the privilege was intended to be temporary only. Within 40 days he had to appear before the Coroner, and there, dressed in sackcloth, he confessed his crime and abjured the realm.

"This hear thou, Sir Coroner, that I . . . of . . . am a . . . (robber of . . . or a murderer of . . .) and a felon of our Lord the King of England, and because I have done many such eviles in this land I DO ABJURE THE LAND of our Lord . . . King of England,

"And I shall haste me towards the port of . . . which thou hast given me . .

"and I swear that I shall not go out of the highway, and if I do, I will that I be taken as a . . . and a felon of our Lord the King;

"and that at such a place . . . I will diligently seek for passage, and that I will tarry there but one flood and one ebb, if I can have passage;

"and unless I can have it in such a place, I will go every day into the sea to my knees, assaying to pass over;

"and unless I can do this within 40 days, I will again put myself into the Church as a . . . and a felon of our Lord the King . . .

"So help me God and His holy judgment."

Then he was required to kiss the book.

Immediately after his confession, and before the abjuration, the Coroner branded a letter A on the brawn of the right thumb with a hot iron "to the intent that he might be the better known among the King's subjects to have abjured." Should the offender fail to confess within 40 days and continue in the sanctuary, any person furnishing him with provisions was guilty of felony.

"What, I wonder" (says H. V. Morton) "has happened to the ghosts of all the fugitives who sought sanctuary there?

"The records in Beverley prove that in 60 years (1478 to 1539) 186 murderers, 208 debtors, 54 thieves, and over 500 other criminals came clamouring at the great sanctuary knocker as if the devils of hell were after them, as they were, no doubt. Some of these fugitives came from London, I wonder why. Were they cut off from nearer sanctuary at the time of their crimes, or did they believe that St. John of Beverley would give them greater protection?"

If there was a sanctuary knocker it has long since disappeared. Many Churches had such knockers, and it is quite possible that there was originally a knocker or a bell on the great door of the Minster. Where such knockers existed a small room was usually built over the door for the accommodation of those clerks whose duty it was to admit the fugitive at any hour of the night. Such a room still exists over the doorway at Beverley Minster.

What an eerie task, sleeping in that small room; waking often to fancy that one heard the running footsteps or the clattering of hoofs; to wait for the frenzied hammering of the knocker or the clanging of the bell, and to hear it reverberating through the empty Church; to go down shivering in the winter night and open the great door, and face the biting wind as the fugitive rushed in, his face turned back to the darkness, and the baffled pursuers . . . !

Rarely, the seeker after sanctuary was a woman. In the long list of those who came; amongst the physicians, the labourers, the dyers, the yeomen, butchers, husbandmen, gentlemen (once it was an Alderman of the City of London) and many more who make up the forbidding list, there is one described as a spinster, and one as a gentlewoman. What circumstances had driven them to violence? Were they debtors? Or were they women who feared the violence of some reckless, dissolute suitor, and felt that the great Minster alone could offer them peace and security? And had they to offer their soft hands to the branding iron, and to give their promise to leave home, and loved ones, and their native country, and to go forth to foreign lands, never to return?

The answer can be read in the records of the Minster.

The gentlewoman, Elizabeth Bewmont, and her husband, Robert Bewmont (probably a schoolmaster) at Heaton (Kirkheaton), came to the Minster on September 26th, 1481, having murdered one Thomas Aldislay, of Aldmondbury, in the same week. "They took the sacrement, according to the custom, and the said Robert and Elizabeth were admitted to the peace." (They were members of the York family of Bewmont).

The spinster, Elizabeth Nelson, of Pollington, in the County of York, had committed the horrid crime of murdering her own infant. She was admitted in the same way.

Those who remained in the great Church of St. John of Beverley bore a strange name, "The Grithmen," or "The Frithmen." This is the story of Sir John Holland, a knight and the King's half-brother, who became a grithman:-

In 1385 an incident which might have had grave consequences to the kingdom happened in Beverley. The Minster had just been rebuilt after the disastrous fire in 1188, and King Richard II. visited Beverley with his Queen, Anne Bohemia, as the King with the Court and an army over 50,000 men were on their way to wage war against Scotland. It is stated by one writer that John Wycliffe, the King's preacher, and much beloved by the good Queen Anne, accompanied the Court.

The King decided to stay three days in the town, and the entire resources of the inhabitants could accommodate only a comparatively minor proportion of the knights and officers, with the result that many gentlemen of the Court had to seek accommodation in the neighbourhood.

Attached to the Queen's train was a young Bohemian knight, Sir Melas, who was trying to obtain lodgings outside the North Bar. His enquiries were voiced in very broken and imperfect English and this was overheard by a squire of Sir John Holland, the King's half-brother. This squire began to ridicule the Bohemian, and eventually ridicule became taunting incivility. One of Sir Ralph Stafford's archers passing by took the part of Sir Melas, and from the incivility the affair quickly developed into a real quarrel. By this time the parties moved into the lane leading to Pighill, and blows were given and returned, with the result that the archer, in retaliation, killed the scoffing squire.

When Sir John Holland learned that his squire was dead, he took a solemn oath that he would neither eat nor drink until he had killed Sir Melas, although the latter was the quite innocent cause of the fray. In his fury Sir John rode down the lane by the dyke side and met Sir Ralph Stafford, who had also been told of the act of his archer-retainer. Sir John Holland mistook Sir Ralph Stafford, the only son of the Earl of Stafford, who commanded the English army, for the Bohemian knight, and struck Sir Ralph with his sword, riding on without stopping to see the result. The blow proved fatal and Sir Ralphs's body was carried through the North Bar to his distracted father, who as senior Earl, was a very powerful noble.

Meanwhile Sir John Holland took refuge in the Sanctuary Chair at the Minster, where the archer who killed the squire in the first affair, and Sir Melas, had also fled for shelter and safety. The Minster clergy then had strange company to look after. The whole Court was in uproar; King Richard swore Holland should die, and would have ordered his immediate arrest and execution, but that the rights of the Frithstool could not be violated even by the King himself.

Joan of Kent, the King's mother, who had been the widow of Sir John Holland's father when she married the Black Prince, the father of Richard II., implored pardon for her elder son on her knees and was so stricken with grief that she lapsed into a swoon which eventually proved fatal.

Things would have been much more entangled had it not been for the forbearance of the Earl of Stafford. After this old soldier had recovered from his first outburst of remorse, he went to the King and told him that until he returned from fighting the Scots he would not think of his bereavement. "I like not, Sire, that the Scots should rejoice at the misery of the Earl of Stafford." When the Scottish campaign was over the old Earl went on pilgrimage to the Holy Land and there died.

Sir John Holland remained as Grithman, or man of the Frithstool, in Beverley, but was ultimately pardoned by the King in view of the death of their mother. Later he was made Duke of Exeter and married one of the daughters of John of Gaunt. The town documents make several references to the grithmen, or sanctuary-men.

"1428. No grithman can be a burgess; nor can he carry any knife or dagger except with a blunted point, nor any club or short sword within the town of Beverley on pain of forfeiture to the Archbishop."

Shortly before Beverley lost its right of sanctuary a law of Henry VIII. (1531) made it compulsory for all grithmen to wear a badge, appointed by the governor of each sanctuary, openly upon their upper garments, of the compass, in length and breadth, of ten inches under pain of forfeiting all the privileges of the sanctuary.

Further, they were forbidden to leave their lodgings except between sunrise and sunset, under penalty of forfeiting their sanctuary for the third such offence.

In 1460 the keepers ordained "That no grithman shall be a burgess, even though he have a royal charter," whilst the burgess oath began, "This swear I, that I am free, and no grithman."

So it went on until the Reformation came, guided by that King of evil memory, Henry VIII., to sweep away, all over Engalnd, the ancient customs, and to curb the power of the great Church which had ruled over England so long. With the coming of the Reformation there disappeared those refuges for the criminal and the fugitive from justice, and the days of sanctuary ended at Beverley. But the old Fridstool still stands there, in the Minster, a silent reminder of the days when the Church could hold the criminal, and defy the law of the land, and when the grithmen, their lives saved, could walk the streets of Beverley, looked at askance by the respectable burgesses, but safe from the consequences of their murders, or robberies, or other sins.

There is a very brief statute of Henry VII. the second passed after his accession to the throne, which recognises the help given to him, in his short, sharp conflict with Richard III., by men in the sanctuaries.

It would seem that many of these men must have risked all by emerging from sanctuary at this time, and taking part with Henry in the campaign which ended on Bosworth Field, and that the new King, immediately he had secured control of the kingdom, generously recognises this help by the issue of a general pardon to "all persons in Sanctuary, and others, who assisted the King in his battle against Richard, Duke of Gloucester, usurper of the realm."

The comment of Mr. J. R. Witty, the authority upon the history of Beverley and its Minster, upon this intervention by the sanctaury men into the civil war, is extremely interesting. He says:-

"This is a very interesting item, previously unknown to me, but in some research on the period I happened to find mention of a Charter of Onspeximus confirming all the privileges of Beverley also dated 2 Hen. VII. 1486.

"Whilst the Corporation did not oppose Edward IV. when he landed at Spurn in March 1471, there is evidence that their sympathies lay with the House of Lancaster, and that the Lancastrian Kings had given very special consideration to the town, and that the efficacy of the Confessor S. John of Beverley was greatly appreciated by the Henry Kings of the fifteenth century. The Percy family had great influence in the town - their Leconfield residence was only a couple of miles away - and the Percy family was definitely for the Lancastrians, and the Towton Field hit the town hardly. Queen Margaret was always popular in Beverley and often visited it.

"Edward IV. was a hard man to the town, and practically emptied its coffers. At this time, too, Hull was definitely filching much trade from Beverley, and it may be that when John de la Pole, who married the sister of Edwartd IV., was named heir to the throne on the death of Richard III.'s son in 1484, the Beverley feeling against de la Pole's Hull became intensified, and this would tend to throw any weight they had, as the second town in Yorkshire then, towards the Earl of Richmond (Henry VII.)

'Henry VII. certainly did something practical for Beverley, and I have a copy of an oath to be taken by the 'worthies' about 1486-1490.

"'I swear to be true and faithful to the XII. Keepers of Beverley for the time being, and to the Corporation of XXX. governing the town. At all times whenever they require advice or assistance for any matter concerning our Lord the King, or our Lord the Archbishop of York, or the community of this Town, I will be prepared with my best counsel and aid, according to my power, and I will keep secret the counsels and discussions of the same community and will not reveal them, So help me God and these Holy Gospels."

Usually and up to this time I do not recall the King being definitely mentioned in the 'worthies' oath.

It is only conjecture, but it may be that the great influx of sanctuary men had become a town's problem, and the frequent mention of squads of troops sent out of the town on various military "jobs" provided one way out of the difficulty. Such may have happened in 1485."

WHIPPING-POST, WANDSWORTH

CHAPTER IX.

DEODANDS

In the very early days vengeance, responsibility and punishment were not thought of as only limited to human beings. The Mosaic law, "If an ox gore a man or woman that shall die, then the ox shall be surely stoned, and his flesh shall not be eaten" (Exodus 21: v.28) lays down the principle that the ox must be punished, for the death it has caused. Here, then, nearly fifteen hundred years before the time of Christ, there is the "deodand"—something which must be given up to God, a proposition accepted by the English law until less than a century ago. If the ox were the property of the dead man, his relatives lost the ox, part of his property; if it were the property of another person, he likewise, lost it, even if he were entirely guiltless in the matter of the death.

Long afterwards, in the laws of Plato, the onus of prosecuting the "slayer" was laid upon the kinsman; the wardens were to try the cause against the animal, and, if condemned it was slain by them, and, a thousand years after the time of Christ, the laws of Alfred contained a somewhat similar provision - "If, at their common work" (of cutting down trees) "one man slay another, unwilfully, let the tree be given to the kindred."

By this time the theory had progressed, and the offending property was now to be devoted to charity. In this case, it will be observed, the loser was not the wood-cutter who had "unwilfully" killed his fellow-workmen, but the owner of the tree, probably the lord. This was unfortunate for the lord, but later lords did very well out of "deodands." Originally it was intended that the forfeited animal or personal chattel should be handed to the King, to be applied to pious uses, and distributed in alms, but English Kings were practical men, where there were possibilities of augmenting their incomes, and the custom grew up of letting out the right to deodands to the lords of the manors or other liberties. The King took a fee for this concession, and did not enquire too closely as to whether the proceeds of the deodands reached the poor or stayed in the lord's pocket.

The usual mass of queer legal decisions ultimately clustered around the law of deodands—if a youngster fell off a cart, not in motion, the cart was safe, but if an adult fell from it and was killed, the cart was forfeit. The great Blackstone laid it down that "where a thing not in motion is the occasion of a man's death, that part only which is the immediate cause is forfeited; as if a man be climbing up the wheel of a cart and is killed by falling from the wheel, the wheel only is forfeited." On the other hand, if the cart was moving, both cart and load were lost to the owner. Again, if a man riding on the shafts of a wagon fell off and broke his neck, horses and wagon were confiscated, but not the load, because it in no way contributed to his death, but if he were run over by the waggon and load, presumably the load would be forfeited, as it had contributed, by its weight, to crushing him to death.

It was all delightfully interesting to the lawyers, but the original idea which lay behind the English law—that the proceeds should be used as an expiation of the sins of those suddenly snatched away in violent death—seems to have receded well into the background.

The finding of a jury was necessary to constitute a deodand, and the death must take place within a year and a day of the accident. The investigation as to the value of the instrument by which death was caused became of some importance, because, upon the verdict of the jury depended the amount received by the claimant, and, as juries did not like deodands, verdicts for trifling amounts were given, in later years, so as to defeat what they regarded as unjust claims.

In all indictments for homicide, the instrument of death, and the value, were presented and found by the grand jury (for instance, "that the blow was given by a certain bludgeon, value 9d.") so that the Crown or the grantee might claim the deodand, for it was no deodand unless presented as such by the jury.

It is an astonishing fact that the belief that beasts, or trees, or inanimate objects could be sufficiently animate to assume a kind of guilt and free will existed until August, 1846. In the sixteenth century a great lawyer Coke (1552-1634) pleaded that a ship in salt (not fresh) water was helpless, because it was subject to dangers upon the raging waves in respect of the wind and tempest, and that it should be therefore, exonerated!

The law of deodand ultimately became, as stated in the preamble to the Act 9 and 10 Victoria, c.62. "unreasonable and inconvenient" so it was abolished in the following words:-

"That from after the First day of September One thousand eight hundred and forty-six there shall be no Forfeiture of any Chattel for or in respect of the same having moved to or caused the Death of Man; and no Coroner's Jury sworn to inquire, upon the sight of any dead body, how the Deceased came by his Death, shall find any Forfeiture of any Chattel which may have moved to or caused the Death of the deceased, or any Deodands whatsoever; and it shall not be necessary in any indictment or inquisition for homicide to allege the Value of the Instrument which caused the Death of the Deceased, or to allege that the same was of no value."

So that was the end of deodands, and the superstitious trials of oxen, and swords, and hatchets, and trees; of Kings trading them out to lords, and, later, juries sitting solemnly to decide their values, and how cheaply they could value them!

CHAPTER X.

THE GALLOWS AND THE GIBBET

A writer of the eighteenth century described London as "The City of the Gallows." "Enter it at any point," he said, "and you will have to pass under a line of gibbets. Pass up the Thames, there were the gibbets along its banks, with the rotting remains of mutineers or persons who had committed murders on the high seas, hanging from them in chains. Land at Execution Dock and the gallows was being erected for the punishment of some offender of the same class.

"Enter from the West, by Oxford Street, and there was the gallows-tree at Tyburn. Cross any of the heaths, commons, or forests near London, and you would be startled by the creaking of the chains from which some gibbeted highwayman was dropping piecemeal. Nay, the gallows were set up before your own door in every part of the town—Kennington Common, Fleet Street, The Strand, Bow Street, Finsbury, The Haymarket, Old Street. After the riots of 1780 the gallows were carried about, and suspected persons hanged on the spot . . . . In short, the law-makers contrived, in the hope of checking crime, to invest its punishment with as many appalling features as possible. In 1752, murders had become so frequent that an Act was passed providing for the execution of every criminal one day after the passing of the sentence and ordering his body to be handed over for dissection at the Barber-Surgeons' Hall, Old Bailey.

But, notwithstanding all this, crime increased."

Hanging, as a method of capital punishment, has been in existence in England from Anglo-Saxon days and a very early print shews that the criminal was hanged by a rope from a cross-bar fixed to two lofty uprights, and later prints shew that this type of gallows continued to be used for centuries. In early days it would appear that the victim was drawn up by the rope and strangled, but in later times a platform appears to have been used, from which the condemned man was compelled to jump into space, or the cart in which he stood was drawn away.

The gibbet, on the other hand, was mainly used for the public display of the bodies of those executed, and chains, iron bands, or an iron contrivance which contained the whole body, were used to suspend the remains from the gibbet. There seems to be some evidence that the gibbet was also used on occasion as a method of execution, the wretched criminal being left to die of exposure and starvation.

In ancient days Yorkshire appears to have been well furnished with these instruments of death, for in addition to the state gallows and gibbets, there were others owned and freely used by the great lords, by some of the towns, and even by the religious houses.

The competition in killing was so keen that in 1278, Edward I. intervened

THE PILLORY

THE COLESHILL PILLORY
(Photo obtained through the courtesy of the Warwickshire Police)

and appointed a commission to enquire into the state of affairs. The Commissioners found 94 of these privately-owned gallows and gibbets in Yorkshire, but this list was far from complete. The citizens of York owned one; the Dean of York owned another. The Abbot of York felt that he should have one, and his example was followed by the Archbishop.

In Howdenshire, the Templars of South Cave carried out their own executions, and even such small communities as Wath and Sherburn, Appletreewick and Laughton, had their own gallows. Settle had both gallows and gibbet.

There were famous gallows or gibbets at Hull and Halifax. At Hull the punishment was inflicted at low-water mark so as to be within the jurisdiction of the Admiralty, the Chief Officer of which, the Admiral of the Humber, was, from the year 1451, the Mayor of Hull. The gibbet at Halifax was a form of guillotine. The Frenchman, Guillotin, who gave his name to this type of machine, really introduced it from England and Scotland, where it had been in use for centuries, and it was first used in France during the Revolution of 1792. It was certainly used in Scotland under the name of "The Maiden" in the sixteenth and seventeenth centuries, and at that time Halifax gibbet was already in use.

In one of his delightful books on England, "The Call of England," H. V. Morton gives an interesting account of the method by which the gibbet was used. "In the sixteenth century." he says, "Hull and Halifax put down this crime with the greatest severity, and punished the criminals with death. In Halifax they erected a guillotine worked by a horse. The horse was harnessed to a rope attached to a sharp knife. When he walked away from the guillotine the knife slowly mounted to the top of the scaffolding. The coiners and coin cutters then placed their heads on the block; someone cut the rope, and the knife came down . . . So you see, the saying, 'From Hell, Hull and Halifax, Good Lord deliver us!' became a very earnest line in the beggars' litany."

This description of the Halifax Gibbet exactly agrees with an illustration given in "Bygone Punishments," and with a very old book "Halifax and its Gibbet Law" (1708).

The gibbet is referred to in a still earlier book, printed before 1600, called "Thomas of Reading." In this book the invention of the gibbet is attributed to a friar, and it is stated that the privilege of hanging which had been given by the King to Halifax "was nothing worth, because when they found any offender, they could not get a hangman to execute him," and then follows the statement about the friar: "and how by a friar a gin was devised to chop off men's heads of itself."

If the offender had been convicted of stealing ox, or sheep, kine or horse, it was laid down that "the self beast or other of its kind shall have the end of the rope tied somewhere unto them, so that they being driven, do draw out the pin, whereby the offender is executed."

It was further ordained that the offender must have been taken in the liberty of the Forest of Hardwick, and if he escaped out of it (the boundary ran about 500 yards away from one side of the gibbet) he could not be brought back. A thief named Dinnis did escape in this way, and never returned into the liberty. He is said to have been seen going away from the direction of the gibbet, and was asked if Dinnis was not to be beheaded that day. His answer was, "I trow not."

A man named Lacy was not so wise. He escaped from Halifax, and for seven years resided out of the liberty. Venturing back again he was seized, and this time the sentence was duly carried out, in the year 1623.

In an appendix to "Halifax and its Gibbet Law" it is said that the mound was re-discovered about 1840 and laid bare, as in the original state, and that steps were taken to preserve it. The mound was about thirteen feet square, and four feet in height, and faced on each side with stone walling. On the higher side was a flight of four or five well-worn steps which the criminal, his executioner and attendants would have to ascend.

The parish register at Halifax contains a list of 49 persons who suffered death on the gibbet, the earliest date being the 20th day of March 1541.

The last occasion on which the Halifax Gibbet was used was in April, 1650, when two men, Wilkinson and Mitchell were executed for thefts of cloth, and two colts. They were evidently executed on the evening of the day on which they were sentenced, for the Church Register gives their burial on that day (30th April).

Combe gibbet stands amongst the prehistoric earthworks on the summit of the Downs at the junction of Hampshire and Berkshire. It is actually embedded in one of the great barrows, or burial places, which abound upon these hills.

On March 7th, 1676, George Brommam and Dorothy Newman were hanged and gibbetted on this gibbet for the murder of the woman's two children. A third child, a boy, overheard the murderers making their arrangements for the murders and escaped. It was upon his information that the man, and the boy's mother, were convicted.

To-day the gibbet, standing over 1,000 feet high, with the wind ever moaning through its outstretched arms, is a sinister symbol of an empty countryside. Once it looked out over prosperous farms—now it broods over one vast rabbit warren.

Another tradition of the gallows is that a father and two sons, gypsies and drovers, were, in different years, hanged here, and their bodies left to decay, for horse stealing.

There is a quaint entry in the Corporation ledgers at Wallingford (Berks.) which dates the erection of the gallows there:-

"9th February, 1636. There was a commission under the broad seal of England, sent to Mr. Mayor from the Lieutenant, and was proclaimed in the Market Place, to erect, build, or set up, either gibbet or gallows within the liberties of the town, and thereupon to execute martial law upon any soldiers that should offend or deserve the same; which bred a good deal of peace amongst us, thanks be to God."

Why the town had to bear the expense of the gallows, in order that military executions might be carried out, is not clear, but the Mayor, Aldermen and Burgesses appear to have been thankful for the privilege!

There was a castle in the town, which was garrisoned, and the soldiers may have given so much trouble that, possibly, the Town Council petitioned the King for special powers.

Pepys, in his famous diary (page 6) refers to the Cheapside gibbet thus"— "January 25, 1660. Coming home I hear that in Cheapside there had been but a little while before a gibbet set up, and the picture of Huson hung upon it in the middle of the street."

This must have been a temporary gibbet to relieve the feelings of the Government over the escape of John Huson, a shoemaker, who had risen to be a Colonel in the Parliamentary Army, and who had sat in judgment upon King Charles. It was probably for the latter offence that he was wanted, but having been warned in time, he escaped to Holland, and died in Amsterdam in 1662.

CHAPTER XI.

HANGING AT TYBURN.

Tyburn Fields, in which stood a grove of old trees, and which was situate at the corner of Edgeware Road and near where Marble Arch now stands, was the most famous public hanging place in London for many centuries.

In the sixteenth century, when the population of London, and, therefore, the number of hangings, was comparatively small, these trees were utilised as gallows. The place took its name from the small Tyburn stream which ran near the spot. Presumably it still runs through London, though now underground. It entered the Thames somewhere near the present site of Buckingham Palace. Originally these Middlesex gallows were known as Tyburn tree, and Connaught Square is claimed as the exact site, but so long as the gallows was a permanent structure it stood, as already stated, at the corner of Edgeware Road, where it joined Bayswater Road.

It was a place of execution as early, possibly, as the end of the twelfth century. Much later, (in 1759) a movable gallows replaced the permanent erection. On some occasions its two uprights and cross-beam are said to have actually spanned Edgeware Road. Several persons could be hanged at one time, and round the gallows were erected open galleries, the seats in which were let, on the occasion of important executions, at high prices. The lives of many well-known offenders ended at Tyburn—Perkin Warbeck, the Pretender (1449); the Nun of Kent (1535); Haughton, last Prior of Charterhouse (1535); John Felton, murderer of the Duke of Buckingham (1628); Jack Sheppard, the highwayman (1724); and the Earl Ferrers (1760). Two Yorkshire Abbotts, those of Jervaulx and Fountains Abbey, hung side by side in the terrible persecution carried on by Henry VIII. at the suppression of the monastaries.

In 1661, the skeletons of Cromwell, Ireton and others of the so-called regicides, were hung upon the gallows, a characteristic gesture of the Stuart Government.

The first execution expressly mentioned as having taken place at Tyburn was that of William FitzOsbert in the reign of Richard I. (1196). He led a rebellion of the poorest citizens of London, which was easily crushed. He was commonly called "Longbeard" and was a lawyer, and had attained such popularity with the lower orders that 52,000 of them bound themselves to obey his orders. After his execution, the gibbet on which the body was exhibited was stolen by his followers, who "paid the same veneration to it as to the cross, and who were equally zealous in propagating reports of the miracles wrought by it."

Near the Tyburn gallows was the military execution ground within Hyde Park. John Rocque's map of London, published in 1746, shows this latter ground marked out, with the description "where soldiers are shot."

The prisoner was conveyed in the death cart from Newgate to the place of execution. There were two places on the journey at which old customs were observed. As the death cart neared the Church of St. Sepulchre, the sexton, in pursuance of the directions contained in a charitable bequest, tolled the bell, and pronounced an admonition to the condemned man to make his peace with God. There was a brief pause at the gate of the Church; the clergyman said prayers for the unfortunate criminal, and, at the same time, the passing-bell tolled its mournful notes.

At the Hospital of St. Giles-in-the-Fields, it was customary for the procession to stop, and the condemned man was presented with a glass of ale. After the hospital was dissolved, this custom was continued at a public-house in the neighbourhood.

A similar custom was kept at York. It gave rise to the saying, "The saddler of Bawtry was hanged for leaving his liquor," and commemorates the story of a condemned man who, refusing to stop to drink his bowl of ale, was executed, his reprieve, which was in the hands of the messenger not far away, arriving just too late to stop his execution.

Rafael Sabatini has written a vivid description of the last ride to Tyburn— "The driver stood up and turned to the prisoner. He held a length of whipcord in his hand, and with this he pinioned the doomed man's wrists behind his back. Then he took up a length of hempen rope with a running noose in it, and deftly flicked the noose over the captain's head, leaving the end of the rope to hang behind him. That done—and with the utmost nonchalance, the ruffian puffing, meanwhile, a short and very foul pipe—the gates were opened.

"The Sheriff's Deputy, a splendid figure in a gold-laced, scarlet coat, gave the word of command, and the procession formed up and started.

"Ahead went the military in their red coats and mitre-shaped hats, opening a way with their musket-butts through the mob that had collected about the prison gates. Out into that seething, human ocean rolled the cart . . . .

"They pushed on. Crowds everywhere along the cart's way; every window held a little mob, assembled to see a man pass to his death . . . .

"The cart at a snail's pace was crawling up Holborn Hill, and everywhere surged the same brutal unfeeling crowd, staring, shouting, jesting. Do not suppose that in this was any political rancour. Few indeed had any notion of the offence for which the Captain was to suffer. He was just a man going to be hanged, and a man going to be hanged was ever an interesting, and often a somewhat amusing spectacle . . .

"They were trundling downhill now, the mob growing more and more dense, the houses thinning. Below, at the Hill's foot, the ground was black with swarming humanity, and from the midst of it, a dark triangular object reared itself—the sinister triple beam.

"As the cart bearing Captain Gaynor came under the fatal beam, the vociferations of the crowd abated. They sank to a mere murmur, to a subdued whisper, as of a breeze stirring through a forest, and lastly into an absolute and deathly silence—the impressive expectant hush of nature when a storm impends.

"The ordinary was reading aloud the Office for the dead. Jack Ketch, the ruffianly driver of the cart, was on his feet. He took the end of the rope that hung from the noose around Captain Gaynor's neck, swung it a moment to gather the required momentum, then threw it over the beam, and deftly caught it as it came round and down. In an instant he had knotted it. In another he had resumed his seat, taken up his whip, and with a sudden stinging cut sent his horse at a half-gallop down the lane which the military had opened out for him in the mob . . .

"Between two of the three uprights of that triangular structure, the body of Captain Gaynor swung gently to and fro, as if the warm summer breeze made sport of it.

At the foot of the gibbet there was an open square, maintained by a hedge of men in scarlet coats and mitre-shaped hats. The drums had long since ceased to beat.

"Came a sharp word of command, and a line of muskets flashed up, and rattled to rest, each upon the shoulder of its owner; another word of command and the redcoats manoeuvred into marching order, four abreast. Then the drums rolled out again, and the scarlet phalanx swung briskly away through the tumultuous crowd.

"The show was at an end.

"Into the open square which the military had maintained at the gallows' foot sprang now some half-dozen resolute and bustling ruffians. The crowd surged after them, like waters released, and a cart pressed forward with the foremost.

"The tallest of these ruffians, with a knife between his teeth, shinned up one of the vertical timbers and threw a leg over the cross-beam from which the body was swinging. With his knife he slashed through the rope, and the body tumbled into the arms of his companions below. Two of them bore it away. They gained the cart, flung in their limp burden, and as one of them vaulted after it, the driver cracked his whip, and cursed the people volubly and obscenely. A way was reluctantly opened, and into this the cart pressed driven forward like a wedge. Slowly it won through . . . "

("The Gates of Doom.")

The body snatchers who had seized the body (the friends of the dead man having made no arrangements for the burial, and the State taking no part in this) sold it to the surgeons for dissection, and the continuation of Sabatini's story is based upon the fact, which appears to be fairly proved from several sources, that, occasionally, the executed man came to life again. There are at least two cases in which the victims of Tyburn were found, when actually on the dissecting table, to be alive. Sabatini gives references to three such cases.

There was no drop in those days (the story is laid at some date after 1745) and it is conceivable that as death was by asphyxiation, and not from a broken neck, there was a possibility that powerful neck muscles, or a very resistant windpipe, might enable a man to emerge alive from such an ordeal.

In the year 1784, the place of execution was changed to Newgate. It was hoped that better facilities would thus be afforded to the public to witness the horrible and degrading spectacle. The moral benefit to the remainder of the prisoners in Newgate was also in the thoughts of those responsible for the change, as, it was said, "they will derive a useful lesson of duty and obedience, and a strong admonition to repentence from the presence of the heavy hand of justice so near the walls."

Charles Dickens, who had witnessed these horrible exhibitions, addressed a letter to "The Times" (November 14th, 1849) in which he took a very different view. He said: "I am solemnly convinced that nothing that ingenuity could devise to be done in this city, in the same compass of time, could work such ruin as one public execution, and I stand astounded and appalled by the wickedness it exhibits."

In 1864, a Royal Commission sat to enquire into the question of public executions, and as a consequence no execution has taken place, in the view of the public, since 1868, when Michael Barrett underwent a public execution for his share in organising a terrible explosion outside Clerkenwell Prison. The outrage was one of those carried out by the Fenians, the wall of the prison being blown down by gunpowder. Twelve persons lost their lives and nearly 120 were injured.

Mr. Samuel Pepys, in his Diary (page 145) has an interesting and characteristic note upon hanging:—

"February 27. 1662. Dr. Scarborough took some of his friends, and I went with them, to see the body of a lusty fellow, a seaman, that was hanged for robbery.

"It seems one Dillon, of a great family, was after much endeavour to have saved him, hanged with a silken halter this Sessions (of his own preparing), not for honour only but it being soft and sleek it do slip close and kills, that is, strangles presently, whereas, a stiff one do not come so close together and so the party may live longer before killed.

"But all the doctors at table conclude that there is no pain at all in hanging, for that it do stop the circulation of the blood, and so stops all sense and motion in an instant."

Note-
"The Hangman's Record" gives two instances of survival after hanging. Both appear to be additional to those quoted by Rafael Sabatini in "The Gates of Doom." They are:
"January 19 1728
Margaret Dickson, for infanticide, executed at Edinburgh. After hanging the usual time the body was being conveyed in a coffin by cart towards Musselburgh. While the driver was taking refreshment at Pepper Hill, the supposed defunct criminal opened the coffin and got out to the surprise and dismay of all who beheld her. Her innocence was afterwards clearly established."
"November 1740.
William Duell, for murder, executed at Tyburn. Duell came to life again when the knife was applied to him in the dissecting room, after being inanimate for three hours. He was eventually transported."

CHAPTER XII.

THE PILLORY

The Pillory was abolished in the year of Queen Victoria's accession to the throne. How long it had existed in England cannot be stated with any certainty. It may have been used in Roman days; certainly it was in use under the name of the "healfang" or "stretchneck" in Anglo Saxon times, and right down to 1837 it was extensively employed. Lords of the manor, heads of religious houses, and every town and village owned, and freely used, the pillory, while the State, by severe penalties, ensured that it should be kept in good order ready for use. Some of the ancient corporations only retained their rights to hold public markets upon the condition that the pillory in the market place was maintained and always ready for use.

Although some attempt was usually made to maintain order and to protect the victim, while he was undergoing his sentence, by the presence of constables or soldiers, imprisonment in the pillory became, in fact, a trial by the public. The criminal who had the sympathy of the mob knew that he had little to fear from the public. Daniel Defoe (the immortal author of "Robinson Crusoe" and writer of scores of other works long since forgotten) was sentenced, 1703, to pay 200 marks; to stand in the pillory three times; to be imprisoned indefinitely and to find sureties for his good behaviour for seven years, for an attack upon the Church. He was so popular with the people that they garlanded him in the pillory with flowers and sang a hymn, "The Hymn to the Pillory," which he had composed in prison. A few years later a public informer (who had sworn falsely against accused persons in order to obtain the reward offered by the State for the conviction of criminals) died in the pillory at Seven Dials, stoned to death by the infuriated populace. Sir Walter Besant, in "The Orange Girl," has written a terrible story of the pillory.

"The punishment of the pillory hands a man over to the people for judgment and execution, for acquittal or for pardon. The law says, 'We find him guilty; it is for the people to increase the punishment or to protest against it.' To look down upon thousands of faces, and to see no gleam of relenting upon one; not one with a tear of pity; to hear their yells of execration; to see the arms spring up with one consent—poor wretch! . . . .

"It took a quarter of an hour to get him up the steps to the platform; another ten minutes before he was placed in the machine, his face towards the crowd, his helpless hands stuck through the holes. When he was ready the Under Sheriff and the constables ducked their heads and ran . . . With a roar as of hungry beasts the mob began . . . sharp flints, stones, brickbats . . . they broke through the line of constables and filled the open space . . . I think they were mad . . . there was neither pause nor cessation . . . I can never forget the sight of the bowed head at which a mob of thousands hurled everything they could find . . . "

93

Such was in many cases, the punishment of the pillory down to the days of only a century ago, when our grandfathers were little boys, and heard the story from their fathers, or even saw a man endure such punishment.

Occasionally the sentence of the Court ordered that an offender should be exhibited in more than one pillory. James Ollerton, of Bowling, a barrator ("a common mover of suits and quarrels in disturbance of the peace; never quiet, but at variance with one another . . . .") apparently carried out his "suits and quarrels" until some enterprising person decided to deal with him as a public nuisance. James was accordingly brought before the Leeds Sessions 1677, and the Court decided to make an example of him. He was ordered to be placed in the pillories of Leeds, Bradford and Halifax, on the next market days, with a paper set on his head bearing the words, "James Ollerton, common barrator," and then to be conveyed to York Castle unless he found sureties for seven years.

A variation of the sentence to stand in the pillory is recorded in the case of Sarah, wife of Mathew Lund, Wakefield, in April 1780. Sarah was ordered to stand, not in the pillory, but on the market Cross at Wakefield—it was unfortunate, from the lady's point of view, that her public appearance was to be on a market day, when the market place would be crowded—for one hour, with a paper, to be conspicuously attached to her, bearing the words "Common Scold."

Another case in which three markets are mentioned, but the sentence does not state whether the prisoner was to stand on the Market Cross or in the pillory, is that of George Metcalfe, of Askrigg. This man was probably a vagrant, for his offence was one of "forging a pass with two Justices' names," vagrants in those days (this was in 1655) having to obtain a pass from a Justice to carry them to the next town. This unfortunate vagabond was sentenced to stand in Beadal, Richmond and Middleham markets on successive market days, with the forged paper in the front of his hat.

Samuel Pepys, that industrious recorder of many interesting incidents in London between 1659 and 1669, tells a brief story which illustrates the forcible methods of the London apprentice of that time: "March 26. 1664. Sir W. Batten tells me how, upon occasion of some 'prentices being put in the pillory to-day for beating of their masters, or such like thing, in Cheapside, a company of 'prentices come and rescued them, and pulled down the pillory: and they, it being set up again, did the like again."

From these instances it will be gathered that many kinds of offenders passed through the pillory—authors, public informers, scolds, vagrants, barrators—and this form of punishment was also used against those in certain trades who committed offences against the public. The baker, for instance, who sold bread which was short in weight, was to stand in the pillory, "which," the statute says, "shall not be remitted to the offender either for gold or silver."

A butcher, also, who sold swine's flesh "measled" (presumably spotted), or flesh dead of the murrain, or that buyeth flesh of the Jews and selleth the same unto Christians," was to be "grievously amerced" for the first time: the second time he was to suffer judgment of the pillory; the third time to be imprisoned and fined, and the fourth time he was to leave the town.

The pillory was the punishment, too, for the brewer who failed to keep the "Statute of bread and ale." He was to be fined three times, but for the fourth offence to be "set upon the pillory, without redemption by money."

At Hull, in the year 1556, the town ordinances laid down that any person taking brick or stone from the town walls should stand in the pillory, and pay a fine of 40 shillings.

The combined pillory, whipping post, and stocks at Wallingford, now in the custody of Major F. R. Hedges, of Wallingford Castle, Berkshire, took the place of earlier pillories which dated back so far as the year 1231. Mr. John Kirkby Hedges, the author of "The History of Wallingford," found an item in the town's accounts for that year for the repair of the pillory.

"It will be seen," he says, "that this terror of evil doers, which occupied a conspicuous position in the Market Place, on the west of the Town Hall, was designed to hold four delinquents, namely:—

"Two in the stocks.

"One at the whipping post.

"One in the pillory at the top."

The building shewn in the photograph is the lower part of the Town Hall in which the dungeon was situated.

The pillory was taken down in 1830. Pillories had ceased to be used for punishment, except in cases of perjury, in 1816. In 1837, the pillory was abolished for all offences. Evidently, no perjuror having been committed to the pillory in the 14 years between 1816 and 1830, the town authorities decided it was time it came down. The stocks remained for many years, but, having fallen into disuse, they also were taken down.

The illustration on page 84 of two men in the pillory shews the type of instrument usually employed. Probably the combination of pillory, whipping post and stocks was adopted in some cases owing to the cost of maintenance being thus lessened.

The Coleshill pillory (Warwickshire) is still standing, and now combines pillory and whipping post. Formerly there were rings on each side of the post, about a foot from the ground (a close inspection reveals that one is still in position on the right-hand side) and with a stool behind, this made an efficient stocks. Higher up on the left-hand side can be seen one of the two rings through which the hands of the victim to be whipped were secured. The pillory itself provides for two victims, side by side. It will be observed that the persons in the pillory were at a considerable distance from the ground. There is one record of a case during Elizabethan times, in another town, in which the small platform gave way, and left the man hanging by his neck and hands. In a subsequent action he was successful in obtaining damages against the corporation owning the pillory.

THREAT OF PILLORY

In the records of the West Riding Quarter Sessions, held at Rotherham on July 14th, 1640, there is a confused and puzzling statement of a case, in which a threat that a man named John Milnthorpe, of Thurgoland, would be put in the pillory, and would lose his ears, was said to have been made by Sir Francis Wortley, a Justice of the Riding.

Milnthorpe was put on oath, and stated that he had been told this by a man named Michael Slack, of the same village.

The Court then drew up a statement, addressed to the Lord Chief Justice and the Judges of the King's Bench, stating that Slack had also been put in the box, and that he had stated that Milnthorpe had said this.

The Court disbelieved Slack, the statement said, and had ordered him to find sureties for good behaviour, but that Sir Francis had intervened in open Court and had asked that Slack should not be bound over, and the Court had, therefore, decided to submit the proceedings to the "wisdom and consideration" of the King's Bench.

The impression left by the story is that Sir Francis had made the threat of the pillory and loss of ears if Milnthorpe refused to give evidence upon some point which affected the Justice, and that Quarter Sessions had decided to discreetly say as little as possible, but wished to be rid of the responsibility for the case.

There is no record of the result of the appeal to the King's Bench.

THE FINGER PILLORY

Instruments of punishment were not always used for the criminal.

Small instruments, called finger pillories or finger stocks, were formerly to be found in old halls, where they were used for the punishment of servants, and even in schools, for the punishment of children. As the name implies, the finger was imprisoned in the pillory—sometimes all the fingers were so secured—and the culprit was as securely fastened as if in the ordinary pillory or stocks.

The finger pillory in the Parish Church at Ashby-de-la Zouch is fitted with a considerable number of holes for fingers differing in size, and when the upper bar was shut down escape would be impossible, whether the offender were man, woman or child.

OTHER FORMS OF THE PILLORY

Punishment in the middle ages was, as a rule, of a barbarous and painful type, and the victim was fortunate indeed if he escaped with his life, but there were exceptions to the rule of cruelty—cases in which, with a sardonic humour, the culprit was made to exhibit himself, and a specimen of his wrong-doing to the public; to hear their free and unfettered comments, and, possibly, to feel

OLD STOCKS AT BINGLEY

97

ASHBY-DE-LA-ZOUCH FINGER PILLORY

their resentment in some more forcible way. They were those forms of wrong-doing from which the public directly suffered, and there was a rough justice in leaving the offending baker or merchant to receive the reprisals with which the community dealt with his offence. The baker, for instance, who gave short weight with his loaves was paraded through the town with samples of his bread tied round his neck. This gave an opportunity to the defrauded housewives to deal with an offence which directly affected the children of poverty-stricken homes, and, of course, was most serious to the very poor.

In the same class was included the fishmonger who sold off his stale fish to the poor. He was punished by being exhibited with a collar of the smelly fish slung over his shoulders. He probably found the odour of his tainted goods more bearable than the jeers and abuse of those who had lost a dinner through his unfair dealings.

In the fourteenth century a grocer who had sold spices which were greatly adulterated, was placed in the pillory, and had the fraudulent mixtures burnt beneath his nose.

The same fate was reserved for the butcher who sold meat unfit for consumption, and, on the other hand, a heretic in the sixteenth century, who had advocated strict Judaism, was committed to prison and ordered to be fed solely upon pork.

The Inquisition had a fitting punishment for the false witness—he was compelled to wear pieces of red cloth, in the shape of tongues, attached to his outer garment, and thus to bear constant, though silent witness to his own sin.

Sometimes a drunkard was compelled to walk through the town encased in a beer barrel with holes cut in the top and sides, through which his head and hands protruded.

This idea of making the punishment fit the crime is not yet dead. An article in the "Justice of the Peace" of March 5th, 1938, under the heading "Modified Pillory" had a paragraph upon a modern method of "pillorying" an offender:—

"A salutory provision which is very little known is contained in the Public Health (London) Act, 1936, section 180(4), whereby a person twice convicted of exposing unsound food for sale, may be held up to public obloquy by having 'a notice of the facts' affixed to his premises for 21 days. This is a healthy way of making the punishment fit the crime. Obstructing the affixing of the notice, or defacing or concealing it while fixed is an offence carrying a penalty not exceeding five pounds. We can imagine an offender being glad to pay the sum to get rid of the notice, or moving away leaving the notice in the air.

"The provision must be very rarely used. Its use at the Old Street Police Court at the instance of the Bethnal Green Borough Council in a recent prosecution is said to be the first occasion, although a similar enactment has been in force 50 years."

CHAPTER XIII.

THE STOCKS

There was an interesting incident, nearly 1900 years ago, which proves that the stocks, as instruments of punishment, were known to the Romans. "And the magistrates rent off their clothes, and commanded to beat them. And when they had lain many stripes upon them, they cast them into prison, charging the gaoler to keep them safely; who having received such a charge thrust them into the inner prison, and made their feet fast in the stocks." (Acts 16: vv. 22-24).

The cheerful prisoners, Paul and Silas, were released by an earthquake, whilst singing praises to God. Judging from the substantial appearance of the stocks used for centuries in every English town and village it would have needed an earthquake to release their occupants. There is no record of any such deliverance![1]

When they were first used in England is not known, but if the Romans were using them in the days of the Apostles, it is quite within the bounds of possibility that they were used during the Roman occupation of this country. Drawings of Anglo-Saxon times indicate that a primitive from of stocks was used in the period between the Roman withdrawal from Britain, and the Norman occupation of the kingdom. That they were in regular use in the fourteenth century is quite clear, for an Act of Edward III., passed in 1351, and known as the Second Statute of labourers, gave power to place unruly workmen in the stocks. The passing of this Act, and the punishment laid down, shews that the stocks were well known at that time. At Wallingford, where the stocks and pillory were combined (see the chapter on the pillory) there is an item in the town's accounts for the repair of the pillory in 1231, and it is quite likely that the stocks even then formed part of the pillory.

The Act of 1351 further enjoined that stocks should be set up in every town between the passing of that Act and the following Pentecost. The Act was not fully carried out, and in 1376 the Commons petitioned Edward III. to order that the stocks should be set up in every village.

It is impossible to give in detail the Acts of Parliament passed in different reigns, but an Act of II Henry VII. (1496) indicates that the punishment of confinement in the stocks, which, in later centuries usually was for a period of hours, was at that time a very severe penalty indeed.

The Act runs thus: "For moderating the provisions of 7 Richard 2, chapter 5, it is enacted that vagabonds, idle and suspected persons, shall be set in the stocks *three days and three nights*, and have none other sustenance than bread and water, and then shall be put out of the town.

"And whosoever shall give such idle person more shall forfeit 12 pence." The Act of Richard II., which is referred to, gave power to deal with vagabonds

[1] * There are other, and earlier references to the stocks in the Bible, e.g. Job 13, v. 27. Job 33, v. 11, and Jeremiah 20, v 2.

and idle persons, in effect, just as the Justice thought fit, and many of the sentences must have been very long ones to necessitate the passing of the moderating Act of Henry VII. Even so, a sentence of three days and three nights, with the the legs held in one position continuously, the victim subject to exposure and hunger, and possibly, the ill-treatment of the ignorant and the cruel, was a very serious punishment indeed.

For centuries the stocks were used as alternatives to prison. In the villages it appears to have been the duty of the constable to be responsible for their renewal and maintenance.

The accounts of many parish constables contain items, such as the following (from the Hooton Pagnall constable's accounts):—

Nov. 2, 1777—Paid John Machin for a pair New Stocks . . . £1 0 6
Paid for a hesp and 2 pr. staples for them 2 0
Spent at setting them down 1 0
Jan. 30, 1789—Paid for a lock for the stocks . . . 1 10
Feb. 12, 1790—For the stocks mending 9 6

The parish constable could place his man in the stocks for temporary confinement until he could bring him before the Justice: drunkards could be ordered to be confined in the stocks for periods of so many hours, and wood-stealers were, in the sixteenth century, placed in the stocks with the stolen wood before them. Vagrants were often placed in temporary confinement in this way, and those found drinking during the hours of Divine Service could be summarily locked in the stocks. In Sheffield on the 12th February, 1790, no less than nine men were thus sentenced to loss of liberty, presumably in small batches, unless more than one set of stocks were employed, for the ordinary type of stocks held two persons only. The stocks at Knaresborough could hold three persons, and, in this case, a stool or bench was provided for the culprits, but in many cases they sat on the bare ground. The Knaresborough stocks are believed to date back to 1300, and must be almost the oldest stocks now existing. A note in an official history states: "When these stocks were last used, they were employed for the detention of debtors. These persons were fastened in them, inside the police station yard, behind iron railings, exposed to the view of the public, and the jeering youths of the town."

It has been claimed that the last Yorkshire stocks to be used were at Stanningley, in which John Gambles, convicted of Sunday gambling, was placed for six hours in April, 1860, but a very interesting letter was sent to the "West Riding Police Journal" (in which these notes on the stocks first appeared) by a reader of the Journal, which appears to give pride of place, in Yorkshire to the Bingley stocks. The letter it will be seen, is dated March 13th, 1866, but we shall never know unfortunately, the name of the person for whom the Inspector held the commitment; the offence for which he had been convicted, nor whether, the stocks duly repaired, the offender unwillingly took his seat in them and endured his allotted period of punishment.[2]

[2] The contents of this letter are reproduced at the end of the chapter.

"The Encyclopaedia Britannica" mentions the Rugby stocks as possibly the last used in England, but the record is, undoubtedly, held by the Newbury stocks, used on June 11th, 1872, for the punishment of one Mark Tuck.

Mr. Walter Money, in his "Popular History of Newbury," describes this rather memorable occasion as follows: "Possibly, Newbury was the last place in England where the stocks were used as a form of punishment, namely in 1872. The stocks, as is well known, are a simple arrangement for exposing a culprit on a bench, confined by having his ankles laid fast in holes under a movable board.

"Previous to the destruction of the old Guildhall in 1828, the whipping post and pillory—one above the other—were placed close to the south side of the building, and the stocks were at the opposite end. The latter were stowed away in the Town Hall cellars, where they had lain forgotten for 14 years. But in 1872 these favourite instruments of punishment devised by the ingenuity of our forefathers, were once more brought into requisition, when one Mark Tuck, an incorrigible bacchanalian, was sentenced to four hours incarceration in the stocks for insobriety and creating a disturbance at the Parish Church. It being a pouring wet day, the stocks were not set up in the Market Place, but placed in the Shambles, while a constable was stationed close by to see that the prisoner was not molested by vengeful missiles or other indignities. Still the punishment was sufficiently severe, for Mark was surrounded the whole time by a crowd of jeering juveniles, to whom the process was a novelty. Mark is reported to have borne up fairly well, fervently ejaculating every time the quarter-hour of the Church clock chimed, 'Thank God, another quarter gone,' at the same time registered it in the accumulated dust of years that still lay thickly upon the stocks. At length the period of incarceration was at an end, and on being released and feeling his feet once more, the victim of this degrading punishment bounded into the police station, almost overturning an old woman in his haste to escape from the sarcastic onlookers.

"Since Mark's involuntary appearance, this interesting relic of 'the good old times' has reposed peacefully in seclusion, and was only brought out at the Art and Industrial Exhibition of 1884, as a specimen of the punishments of a less civilised age."

(The photograph of the Newbury stocks on page 126 is taken with the beautiful door of the ancient Cloth Hall in the background. In this hall, on June 25th, 1811, a memorable record was achieved. Sir John Throckmorton laid a wager of a 1,000 guineas that, between sunrise and sunset on that day a coat should be made, the wool for which had been that morning on the sheep's back.

The proceedings began at five in the morning. The original deed of the presentation of the coat states that "the sheep were shorn, the wool sorted and spun, the yarn spooled, warped, loomed and wove, the cloth burred, milled, rowed, dyed, dried, sheared and pressed. The cloth (which was a Hunting Kersey of the admired dark Wellington colour) having been thus made in 11 hours was put into the hands of the tailors at four o'clock in the afternoon, who completed the coat at 20 minutes past six." The coat was worn the same evening at a dinner.)

During the fierce persecution of the Quakers in the latter part of the seventeenth century, many of the meetings for worship were broken up, and the men and women imprisoned and treated with great cruelty. The children continued to meet, and, in a letter from Bristol to George Fox in 1682, there is a depressing record of the brutalities of the Justices:—

"On the 7th of the month called July they dispersed the meeting, which then consisted chiefly of children, for, the men and women being in prison, the children kept up their meetings regularly, and with a surprising gravity and composure . . . On the 16th, Tilly caused five of the boys to be set in the stocks three-quarters of an hour. On the 23rd, eight of the boys were put in the stocks two hours and a half. On the 30th, about 55 children were at the meeting, when Helliar, with a twisted whalebone stick, beat many of them unmercifully, striking them violent blows on their heads, necks and faces. On the 6th of the month called August, Tilly beat some of them with a whalebone stick, and sent four boys to Bridewell, who were released in the evening with threats of whipping if they met again. He also sent 11 boys and four girls to Bridewell, till a friend engaged for their appearance before the Deputy Mayor next day."

It is stated, on the authority of several writers, that one of the most notable persons ever placed in the stocks was Cardinal Wolsey. About the year 1500, he was the incumbent of Lymington, near Yeovil, and having overstepped the bounds of strict moderation at the village feast, a local Justice, Sir Amais Poulett, a gentleman who took a rather serious view of his duties as a Justice of the Peace, ordered his imprisonment in the stocks.

THE JOUG

The "joug," an instrument used in Scotland more often than the stocks, consisted of an iron collar with joint or hinge at the back for opening and closing, padlocked on the neck of the victim, and usually attached by a chain to the Church door, a market cross, a prison door, or some other public place. This implement probably gave rise to the slang name for a prison, "The Jug."

Some writers use the word "Joug" (there are several spellings— "Jougs," "Juggs," or "Joggs" are other forms of the word) for the stocks, as well as for the instrument described above.

Note— The following is the text of Inspector Croft's letter.

"Court House Bingley
March 18 1866.
Dear Sir,
Will you have the goodness to draw the attention of the Bingley Improvement Commissioners to the state of Repair of the Public Stocks in the Market Place. I hold a Commitment against a person for the Stocks and I am unable to execute it until they are repaired.
I am Your most Obet Servant
(Signed) James R. Croft Inspector of Police.
J. Thacker Esq., Bingley."

CHAPTER XIV.

THE DUCKING STOOL

The history of the ducking-stool goes back, at least, to Norman times, and one of the duties of the Court Leet was to examine the state of repair of the ducking-stool, the pillory and the stocks, but it is extremely likely that the history goes back to far earlier days

The Anglo-Saxons used the tumbrel-pond for drowning and (in cases of lesser offences) ducking women, while, earlier still, the Romans had "fossa" or ducking-pond in use during their occupation of Britain. Whether the "Scealding" or "Scolding" stool of the Saxons was the ducking-stool, or a very early form of the cucking-stool, is not clear.

"The general belief is that the cuck-stool, or cucking-stool, was identical with the ducking-stool, but there was an essential difference and each was used originally for he punishment of different offenders.

"The ducking-stool was employed principally for the correction of scolds, and any woman convicted of persistent scolding was "ducked," not merely because she was a domestic plague, but because she was a public nuisance, who disturbed the peace of the neighbourhood.

"'There stands, my friend, in yonder pool,
An engine called the ducking-stool.
By legal power handed down,
The joy and terror of the town.
If jarring females kindle strife,
Give language foul, or be not wife
If noisy dames should once begin
To drive the house with horrid din—
'Away,' you cry, 'You'll grace the stool,
We'll teach you how your tongue to rule!'

"Sometimes the scold vented her angry clamour as soon as she recovered breath after the first plunge, and then the immersion was repeated until silence was eventually restored—

"'And rather than your patience lose,
Thrice and again repeat the dose,
No brawling wives, no furious wenches,
No fire so hot, but water quenches.'

"This was the function of the ducking-stool, but the cuck-stool was an ancient punishment inflicted upon brewers and bakers who transgressed the laws or gave short weight persistently.

"In the reign of Henry VIII. the cucking-stool was used to punish those, carders and spinners of wool, who were convicted of fraudulently defrauding their customers." (From "Beverley Street Names," by J. R. Witty).

It was also used for scolds as an alternative to the ducking-stool. In the West Riding Sessions records appears the following entry:—

"Dorothy Marwood, wife of John Marwood, of Thorpp Hesle, husbandman, for being there on 1st July, 1639, and at divers other times, both before and since, a common scold, disturber of the King's Peace and calumniator. Witn. Christian Hill, Sam Whitley, Jane Guest. (At large. Doncaster 9th Oct., 1639, the said Dorothy stood 'in the cucking stool' at Wentworth)."

Horsfall Turner in his book, "Wakefield Prison," seems to suggest that the exposure in the cucking-stool was in the nature of an abandonment of the woman to the tender mercies of the public, similar to the pillory. He says "She was exposed by being carried through the village to her own home; tied in a chair without a seat, and the rest must not be stated, so depraved were the exhibitions of those times. But she was not ducked. This parade was sufficiently ignominious to even an immodest woman to be a far greater disgrace than the ducking-stool performance." Later the ducking-stool and the cucking-stool came to mean the same thing, and both terms were used for the ducking-stool.

"The ducking-stool was a fixture over the pond; the cuck-stool was on wheels, and the wrong-doer was exhibited in the machine outside his own premises and in the public market place before being wheeled to the pond and there soused in the muddy and very unpleasant pool."

There was a difference in the treatment of the man brewer and the woman brewer under the Assize of Bread and Ale, the man suffering a pecuniary penalty for his first three offences, and then to stand in the pillory, but the woman to be punished by the tumbril, trebucket or castigatory "if she offends divers times and will not amend." (In other words, the ducking-stool).

The Archbishop of York had his own ducking-stools in his Manors of Otley, York, Beverley, Sherburn and Patrington, and used them, sometimes in defiance of the civil powers.

The punishment at Beverley was of very old standing, for it is mentioned in 1286 as one of the perquisites "of ancient time" of the Archbishop, as overlord of the town.

Sometimes the "stool" took the form of a stout chair, worked by a rope and pulley, and suspended from a movable arm attached to a stout pillar erected on the side of the river or pond, but, in some places, the chair was fastened to the end of a long plank or pole, worked as a see-saw, a rope being fixed to the end on the landward side so that the victim could be quickly pulled above the water again.

Sometimes, however, the ducking-stool was not a fixture, but was mounted on a pair of wooden wheels so that it could be wheeled through the streets to the pond or stream.

Yet another type was a chair on two wheels with two long shafts fixed to the axle.

In sentencing a woman the magistrate ordered the number of duckings she should have.

Sometimes a condition was attached to the sentence, as in the case of Margery Watson, of Whitby, a notorious scold (1657), who was sentenced to be ducked by the constable within a month, unless she publicly asked pardon of James Wilkinson's wife in Whitby Church or at the Market Cross.

There is one unusual case on record in which a husband and wife were ducked together at Kirkby, in Yorkshire, about 1770. The husband had applied for his wife to undergo the punishment on account of her quarrelsome nature, but the magistrate decided that one was no better than the other, and ordered a joint punishment! Back to back, therefore, husband and wife were chaired, and dipped into the cold water of the pond.

In 1602 Katherine Hall and Margaret Robinson, of Wakefield, were ordered, at Wakefield Sessions, to be "soundly ducked" (apparently, in this case, the Justices did not specify the actual number of duckings to be administered). There are scores of other similar sentences in the records of the West Riding Quarter Sessions, and there is no doubt that the ducking-stool was much used, and that it was much feared. The hostile attitude of the crowd undoubtedly could, and did, influence the men employed to administer the punishment, and sometimes the immersion proved too much for the unhappy woman, and she was drawn out of the water dead, or subsequently succumbed to exposure or pneumonia.

The last time the Nottingham ducking-stool was used was in 1731, when the Mayor (Thomas Trigge) caused a female, accused of immorality, to be placed in it and left to the mercy of the mob, who ducked her so severely that her death ensued shortly afterwards. The Mayor was prosecuted for this outrage, but the result of his trial is not known. The ducking-stool was ordered, however, to be immediately destroyed.

There seems to be some conflict as to when the ducking-stool was last used in England. Horsfall Turner says he cannot find any record in Yorkshire after 1745: another writer thinks its use persisted until 1770, but William Andrews gives two instances in the nineteenth century, at Plymouth in 1808, and in 1809 at Leominster. In 1817, a woman was sentenced to be ducked at Leominster, and was wheeled round the town in the chair, but was not ducked, as the water, luckily for her, was too low.

The Ipswich ducking-stool shews a strongly-built chair, now in the possession of an Ipswich family. The second illustration shews the ancient ducking-stool still in position over the River Stour at Fordwich, in Kent, and the photograph shews the rope and pulley by which the chair was suspended from a crane. The history of this ducking-chair suggests that it was used not only for brawling women, but for actual executions by drowning. Executions of criminals were certainly carried out at this point of the river, the victim being immersed until dead. This small municipality also possessed a gallows which stood on the hill above the town.

The punishment of the ducking-stool did not always daunt the confirmed scold. On Saturday, October 14th, 1738, a woman notorious for her quarrelsomc and evil tongue, was ducked in the Thames, in pursuance of a sentence passed upon her at the Kingston-on-Thames Quarter Sessions. But the immersion had so little effect upon her that "had not the officers interfered, she would have deserved a second punishment even before she was dry from the first."

John Howard, in his travels, visited the Liverpool Bridewell in 1782 and discovered that the ducking-stool was being used there for the purpose of giving a compulsory bath to women vagrants. After describing the ducking stool, which appears to have been of the ordinary type—a chair at the end of a long pole—he wrote: "In this all the females (not the males) at their entrance, after a few questions, were placed, with a flannel shift on, and underwent a thorough ducking, three times repeated—a use of the bath which I dare say the legislators never thought of when in their late Act they ordered baths with a view to cleanliness and preserving the health of the prisoners, not for the exercise of a wanton and dangerous kind of severity. But I was glad to find that this use of the bath has been discontinued since my visit."

CHAPTER XV.

WHIPPING

Whipping, or flogging, has always been one of the most common forms of punishment in every country. It was laid down by the Mosaic code. In the East the bastinado, a light bamboo, applied to the feet or body, has been in use for centuries. The Romans used rods, and doubtless brought them to England. In Russia, the fearful instrument known as the knout - thongs and wires interwoven - generally killed its victims by laceration and shock. In England the whip, the birch and the cat-o'-nine-tails have been the most common instruments of flogging. The history of the Army and Navy shews that sentences of even 500 lashes with the cat-o'-nine'-tails were frequent in the last century, and that if the victim did not die under the punishment, he was scarred for life. The well-known saying, "No room to swing a cat around" is supposed to have had its origins in the fact that between decks in the old wooden battleships it was almost impossible to stand upright and that all floggings, therefore, had to take place on deck.

It must be remembered that an organised system of State prisons was unknown in England in past centuries, so that some summary and speedy method of punishment had to be found, hence the universal provision of stocks and pillories, always to be kept ready for use for short terms of detention, and the infliction of whipping which, the sentence carried out, left the sufferer free to go his way. In days when whipping was universal, when masters and mistresses flogged their servants without mercy; and parents and schoolmasters whipped the children frequently and savagely; it is not surprising that the public spared little pity for the vagrant, dragged naked at the cart-tail, and whipped out of the parish or township. Women fared no better than men until the end of the eighteenth century, and even the children of the vagrants shared their parents' sufferings.

The Whipping Act of Henry VIII. (1530) directed that vagrants were to be carried to a market town, or other place, and "there tied to the end of a cart, naked, and beaten with whips throughout such market town or other place, till the body shall be bloody by reason of such whipping."

Later the victim was stripped only from the waist upward, men, women and children suffering thus.

The abolition of the religious houses in the sixteenth century had a very considerable bearing upon the question of vagrancy. Some may have been ill-conducted, and the powerful position held by the Church had for centuries raised diffficult questions, such as the abuse of sanctuary and benefit of clergy, but there is no dispute as to the fact that they were the great relief establishments of former times, and their abolition disclosed how many idle, as well as destitute persons, there were in the country. In an attempt to drive these people off the roads and back to their parishes, statutes against vagrants and sturdy beggars became numerous and severe. It was contended that the former indiscriminate alms-giving of the monasteries had made the labouring population idle and corrupt. On the other hand, apart from the religious orders, thousands and thousands of labourers had been employed by the religious houses, and these men were thrown upon the country, and added to the great army of poverty-stricken and needy men, women and children tramping the country, harried by the Justices and the constables; flogged, branded and imprisoned, in the vain effort to drive them from each parish. Even when they reached their own parishes, their reception, if not a hostile one, was a cold one, for the poor relief system had gone for the time being, and every parish had its own problems.

Little effort to deal with the problem by constructive legislation was attempted in the reigns of Henry's children, Edward VI. and Mary, and it was not until the reign of Elizabeth that the first real attempt to deal with the poor in a rational and humane way was embodied in a statute.

"The terrible measures of repression went on pitilessly; we find the magistrates of Somersetshire capturing a gang of 100 at a stroke, hanging 50 at once on the gallows, and complaining bitterly to the Council of the necessity for waiting until the Assizes before they could enjoy the spectacle of the 50 others hanging beside them. But the Government were dealing with the difficulty in a wiser and more effectual way. The old power to enforce labour on the idle, and settlements on the vagrant classes was continued, and each town and parish was held responsible for the relief of its indigent and disabled poor, as well as for the employment of able-bodied mendicants. But a more efficient machinery was gradually devised for carrying out the relief and employment of the poor. Funds for this purpose had been provided by the collection of alms in Church; but the Mayor of each town, and the Churchwardens of each country parish were now directed to draw up lists of all inhabitants able to contribute to such a fund, and on a persistent refusal the Justices in sessions were empowered to assess the offender at a fitting sum, and to enforce its payment by imprisonment. The principles embodied in these measures, that of local responsibility for local distress, and that of a distinction between a pauper and a vagabond, were more clearly defined in a statute of 1572.

"Overseers were appointed to enforce and superintend their labour, for which wool, hemp, flax or other stuff was to be provided at the expense of the inhabitants; and houses of correction were established in every county for obstinate vagabonds, or for paupers refusing to work at the overseer's bidding . . . . The well known Act which matured and finally established this system, the 43rd of Elizabeth (1601) remained the base of our system of pauper-administration until a time within the memory of living men."

(John Richard Green in "A History of the English People.")

The records of any typical English town of the early part of the seventeenth century, shew clearly how, while the whippings of the vagrants went on, there grew up, side by side with the old cruel system of attempted repression of the poor—deserving and undeserving—a spirit of local charity and greater kindliness to the wayfarers and the destitute while the new poor law system was slowly being carried into effect.

Doncaster, an important market town astride the great North Road, appears to have taken rather unkindly, at first, to the new system of compulsory levy. Tomlinson in his history, says: "I am strongly of opinon that a considerable number of resident occupiers not actually paupers, were exempted, on account of their poor circumstances, from contributing to the rates. According to the first assessment list which I have been able to discover, there were, about the close of the sixteenth century, 134 registered ratepayers, the total amount to be collected in one book being 13/8. How many books were required for the maintenance of the poor in a year is not certified, but the only item above 4d. is one of 1 6d." Many were assessed at 1d. only.

There are scores of entries of amounts paid to the beadles during the first half of the seventeenth century for whipping rogues and idle people, and in every case, the amount allowed to these officials was 4d. per whipping, e.g.:—

Sept. 2, 1614, Paid to Wray for whipping a rogue ... ... 4d.
and, further, there are items for expenses incurred in passing on vagrants to the next town, e.g.:—
April 4, 1632. Pd. to the beadles for conveying a vagrant with a pass ... 6d.
June 2, 1672. Pd. to the beadles for a cripple with a pass ... 6d.

On the other hand, there are many items recording charitable disbursements to some of the great stream of needy people passing up and down the great highway, e.g.:—

1625. Feb. Given to a poor Irishwoman that had 7 children, and had her house and all her goods burned in Ireland ... ... 12d.
Given to two poor men, with a "sorte" of poor children, that had great loss by sea ... ... 12d.
Aug. Given to a soldier with a pass from the States into England, and so to York ... ... 2d.

1626. Apl. Given to a man who had been robbed at sea by the Dunkirks both of ship and goods ... ... 6d.
Sept. Given to a poor sailor that was in a ship off Holland, and was taken by the Dunkirks ... 3d.
(There are several entries of charities bestowed upon victims of the "Dunkirks"—presumably the enterprising and piratical mariners of Dunquerque.)
1631. Feb. To a poor scholar ... ... 4d.
1639. Nov. To three poor Irishwomen with a pass ... 4d.
1640. July. Given to a poor woman that had been robbed by the soldiers. . . 4d.
1639. Sept. Given to a poor gentlewoman great with child ... ... 3d.
1639. Sept. Given to a poor gentleman that had his wife and two children with a pass ... ... 2d.

Sept. Given to Robt. Vicars, sometime servant to Sir Robert Swift, distressed in his passage by Doncaster . . . . . . 1/ -

So that not all who passed through Doncaster, footsore and in great need, were whipped at the whipping post, or at the cart tail. Nor is evidence lacking that the village constable in the eighteenth and nineteenth centuries, was sometimes inclined to be sympathetic to the needy, passing through his village. Hooton Pagnell, a delightful little village some miles out of Doncaster, is a typical rural community, and the accounts of its Parish Constables offer frequent proofs that even such a small community, its population mostly farm and estate labourers, raised no objection to the disbursement by the constable of such items as:—

Jan. 13, 1769. Gave two men with a pass . . . . . . 6d.
Oct. 26, 1775. Paid a soldier with a pass . . . . . . 6d.
Apl. 10, 1783. Paid to two poor sufferers by fire . . . 6d.
Apl. 23, 1807. 7 woman and 9 children with pass . . . 1/6
(At one period a woman acted as Constable in this village. She kept no accounts!)

But in Yorkshire, as in every other county in England, the vagrant had a hard life. In July, 1650, two men at Richmond were stripped to the waist, whipped and sent from constable to constable to their settlement. In 1764, at Wakefield, several beggars were whipped through the market place, and out of the town. Minor offences received the same treatment. Joseph Reiner, of Southowram, and his daughter Jane, for stealing a pan, were ordered to be whipped from the Court House to the Bull Ring at Wakefield, and (although they had committed no offence), two younger daughters shared the same punishment (1681). Even those criminals who went to prison did not escape whipping. In 1736, West Riding Quarter Sessions ordered that the governor of Wakefield Gaol should receive 1/- for each whipping he inflicted, and he was to have "power to punish by moderate whipping disorderly persons and those refusing to work." Doncaster Town Council on May 5th, 1713, ordered the erection of a whipping post at the Butter Cross. Many of the old Corporation records for Yorkshire towns shew items in the accounts for the cost of whippings by constables and beadles, and charges by Churchwardens figure in Church accounts. In the Churchwardens' accounts at Barnsley, in 1622, the following notes appear:—

1622. William Rogers for going with 6 wanderers to Ardsley . . . . . . 2d.
Mr. Garnett, for making them a pass . . . . . . 3d.
Rd. White, for whipping them according to law . . . 2d.
(Presumably the whipping lasted from Barnsley to Ardsley.)

COMBE GIBBET

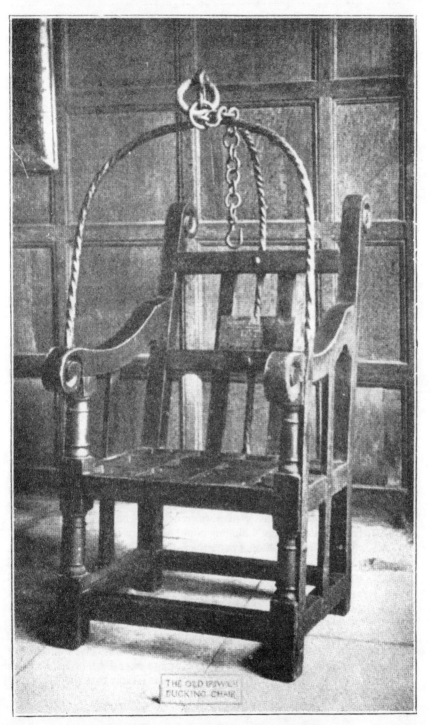

THE IPSWICH DUCKING STOOL

The Wakefield constable's accounts shew that whipping was a lucrative occupation (at Doncaster in the same century, the beadles received only 4d. per whipping):

1787. May 15. Assistance at Whipping 3 men 3/-
July 6. Assistance at Whipping 3 men 3/-
Aug. 17. Assistance at Whipping 2 men 2/-
Sept. 7. Assistance at Whipping 3 men 3/-

After a vagrant beggar had been whipped he was entitled to a testimonial signed by the minister of the parish, and countersigned by the constable, setting forth the date and place of his punishment. This interesting document ran in some such form as this:—

"William Brown, a sturdy vagrant beggar, aged about 35, short of stature and somewhat corpulent, blackhaired, and cross-eyed, left arm torn from his coat and large patch on the seat of his trousers, was this . . . day of . . . 16 . . . . openly whipped at Doncaster in the West Riding of Yorkshire, according to the law, as a wandering rogue, and is assigned to pass forthwith from parish to parish by the officers thereof the most straight way to Oxford in the County of Oxford where he confesseth he was born, and he is limited to be at Oxford aforesaid within twelve days now next ensuing at his peril .

Given under the hands and seals of
Cedric Wilson
Minister of Doncaster aforesaid
Tom Smart
Constable of Doncaster."

If a vagrant was found by a constable without such a pass he was liable to be at once arrested, and to face another flogging. If found incorrigible by the Justices in Quarter Sessions, he could be transported.

If the man carried a pass, he was compelled to produce it, for self-protection, and so each constable knew in which direction he should be proceeding. Once back in the town where his settlement was, he became the responsibility of that township. Taken in conjunction with the fact that many vagrants bore the branded "R" ("rogue"), the pass system was roughly effective.

How terrible a punishment whipping could be is proved by two instances. The sentence passed on Titus Oates, the informer, in the reign of James II., was an extraordinary and savage one, for it included being pilloried twice, and tied to a cart and flogged, first from Aldgate to Newgate, and, after an interval of two days, from Newgate to Tyburn. He was terribly handled in the pillory by the mob, and was in no condition to stand the floggings, but the sentence was carried out and he was mercilessly lashed into unconsciousness. Two days later he was again brought out, this time on a hurdle, as he was unable to stand, and flogged with hundreds of lashes. An eye witness says: "He received upwards of 2,000 lashes. Such a thing was not inflicted by any Jew, Turk or heathen, but by Judge Jeffreys. Had they hanged him they had been more merciful."

Dangerfield, another informer, sentenced to be similarly whipped, from Aldgate to Newgate, and from Newgate to Tyburn, was so shockingly treated that he died later as a result of the flogging. On the way back to Newgate, he was struck across the face with a cane by a man named Francis, the blow destroying the sight of the eye. The Government, which was directly responsible for Dangerfield's death, caused Francis to be arrested, tried upon a charge of murder, and hanged.

Whippings were carried out so late as 1850. Nearly all towns and villages had a whipping post—very often rings were attached to the post of the pillory for this purpose—the cart-tail being used for the vagrant and for cases in which the whipping was ordered to be carried out from one point in a town to another, but whipping in public was done away with in 1817.

The whipping of female vagrants had previously been abolished in 1791. The whipping post is shewn in the illustrations (in the chapter on the pillory) of the Wallingford and Coleshill combined stocks, whipping posts and pillories.

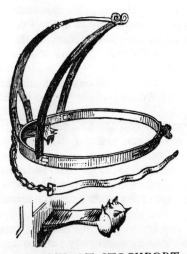

BRANK AT STOCKPORT

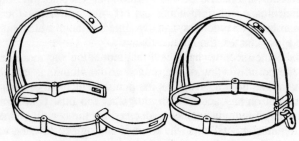

BRANK AT WALTON-ON-THAMES

115

CHAPTER XVI.

MUTILATION

In the olden days a sentence of the pillory was often accompanied by other, and more savage, punishments. Sometimes the ears were nailed to the board containing the hole for the head. Sometimes the nose was slit, and there are many records of cases in which one ear, or both, were cut off. Mr. William Andrews, in his "Bygone Punishments," states that an instrument for cutting off the ears, used in the time of Henry VIII. as a penalty for not attending Church, was to be seen at Playford Hall, near Ipswich. William Prynne (1600-1669), a Member of Parliament, a barrister, and a Puritan, received a sentence (1634) of imprisonment for life; a fine of £5,000, to be expelled from Lincoln's Inn, and to have both ears removed in the pillory. Three years later, he received a fresh sentence. The stumps of his ears were shorn off in the pillory, and he was branded with the letters S.L., meaning "seditious libeller." It is not surprising that, during the Commonwealth, he was an ardent Puritan, but his zeal seems to have so far outrun his discretion that he received several other sentences of imprisonment from the Puritans for his misplaced enthusiasm!

In 1676, Robert Metcalfe, a County Court Bailiff, was ordered to stand in the pillory in Wetherby Market Place, and to have his ears cut, for too harshly carrying out his duties .

Sometimes, by a refinement of cruelty too horrible to dwell upon, the unfortunate in the pillory, having had one or both ears nailed to the board, was left to tear off his own ears in order to secure freedom.

In 1552, a "gentleman" was set in the Cheapside pillory for fraud and one of his ears was nailed to the pillory. When the prescribed period of his sentence had expired "he would not rent his eare and one of the beadles slitted it upward with a penknife to loose it."

It would be impossible in a brief chapter to go fully into the many inhuman ways in which men in power and authority mercilessly tortured those who, in past centuries fell into their power. From the days of the long fight between the Saxons and Danes, when, in one sea battle, the captured sailors all had their noses and right hands cut off—for centuries—there are records of inhuman laws, or practices, usually aimed at the disablement of the criminals of the lower classes, though not always.

The Danes seem to have held that mutilation was more desirable (whether from the point of view of the judges or the victims is not clear) than death. Canute's laws do not favour capital punishment: "We command that Christian men be not on any account for altogether too little condemned to death, but rather let gentle punishments be decreed for the benefit of the people." These "gentle punishments" took the form of cutting off the ears, nose or upper lip, plucking out the eyes, or scalping.

William the Conqueror appears to have taken the same view; certainly the record of mutilations carried out by the Normans is not pleasant reading. The plucking out of eyes and the cutting off of hands or feet, or both, were amongst the dreadful mutilations employed.

Henry II. (1176) for robbery, murder, false coining, and arson ordained that the punishment should be amputation of the right hand and right foot. The ordeal was allowed for thefts under 5/-, but he who failed lost a foot, and, ten years afterwards a hand was struck off.

Striking a blow in a palace or Court of Henry VIII. was punishable by the loss of the right hand.

An Act of Edward VI. (1552-3) laid down the drastic punishment of mutilation for brawling, accompanied by blows, in a church or churchyard, the Church adding excommunication to the punishment. The offender was tried before a jury, and, on conviction, could be sentenced to have one of his ears cut off or, having no ears, to be branded with the letter "F" ("Fray-maker"). This was the law until so late as 1829.

In the thirteenth century, thieves who had stolen more than one shilling were allowed to abjure the realm or to lose a thumb—a cheerless choice for the unfortunate who had to face it. For petty larceny (thefts under one shilling) the offender might lose an ear for the first offence, and his remaining ear for the second offence. When his supply of ears was exhausted the gallows awaited him, unless he could reach the forest or the sanctuary.

Of the ghastly additions to the sentence of hanging for treason which began to make their appearance in this century, little need be said. "Drawing," the second word of the sentence, of course preceded the hanging, for it meant that the wretched man was drawn behind a horse over the roads to the place of execution. As this usually meant that he arrived there dead, or nearly so, a hurdle was used in later centuries. The other horrible details of the mutilation must not be mentioned.

The punishments inflicted during Elizabeth's reign for seditious libel were very brutal. Stubbs, a writer, and Page, a publisher, lost their right hands, the wrist being divided by a cleaver being driven through the joint by the blow of a mallet.

Stubbs showed great hardihood in facing his terrible fate, and Camden in his "Annals of the Year 1581" says: "I remember, being then present, that Stubbs, when his right hand was struck off, plucked off his hat with his left hand, and said with a loud voice, 'God save the Queen.' The multitude standing about was deeply silent, either out of horror at this new form of punishment, or out of commiseration with the man."

It is surprising that men lived after such crude severance of hand or foot, and it would seem that some rough method of cauterisation must have been employed, such as a red-hot iron, to stay the haemorrhage, but there is no mention of this by any of the old writers.

Mutilation was not always inflicted by the State. The Statute of 5 Henry IV., chapter V., for "The punishment of certain mayhems ("mayhem" was the original form of the word "maim") was directed against illegal maimings. It ran as follows: "Also, because that many offenders do daily beat, wound, imprison and maim divers of the King's liege people, and, after, purposely cut their tongues, or put out their eyes; it is ordained and established, that in such cases the offenders who shall cut the tongues, or put out the eyes, of any of the King's liege people, and that duly proved and found, that such deed was done of malice prepensed they shall incur the pain of felony."

The gentlemen who practised the little diversions of tongue-slitting or putting out eyes would certainly observe the loophole in the Act, and were, probably, prepared with a defence that the matter was only a joke, or an accident, or a mistake, and that no malice was intended.

It is impossible to give more than one or two illustrations of savageries perpetrated outside the law, but in 1712, when the efficiency of the London police system was reaching its lowest point, the "Mohocks," a number of young men of the town established a reign of terror in London, the slitting of noses, and the wounding of men and women being amongst their nightly amusements.

The reply of the public to this type of savage lawlessness was to arm themselves, and to set up mantraps and spring guns in their gardens, and their shrubberies and coverts, but so many innocent persons were maimed and killed by these dangerous forms of defence, that in 1827 an Act was passed prohibiting their use.

DONCASTER GAOL (corner of Factory Lane)

CHAPTER XVII

BURNING TO DEATH

Burning to death is a form of punishment which appears in the histories of many European countries, as well as of England.

In very early days arson was regarded with the utmost aversion; the burning of a man's home was easy, for it was built wholly of inflammable materials; the burning of his cornbarn was almost equally serious, for it left him starving; so the penalty was one of retribution—the offender was himself burned to death. A case of this nature is recorded in the days of King John, but the later development of the law led to the substitution of the gallows for the stake.

Burning to death for heresy was often used on the Continent long before it was legalised in England in 1401, but there were isolated cases here before that year. The authority for such a method of putting to death is a matter which may never be satisfactorily settled, but a member of the Albigensian sect was burnt to death in London in 1210, and there is abundant proof that in 1222 a young deacon of the Church, after an ecclesiastical trial, was handed over to the Sheriff of Oxfordshire to be burnt for adopting the Jewish faith for the love of a Jewess. The sentence was immediately carried out.

A number of men and women were burnt in Ireland for heresy, after a trial by the bishop, at which English representatives were present, in 1324.

There were, too, prior to 1401, cases of the burning of alleged witches and sorcerers, but it is after that year that we come to firmer ground.

In 1401, by the Statute of Heresy, the bishops were empowered to arrest all preachers of heresy, all schoolmasters infected with heretical teaching, all owners and writers of heretical books, and to imprison them, even if they recanted at the King's (Henry IV.) pleasure. Failure to abjure enabled the bishops to hand over to the civil officers, and by these— "so ran the first legal enactment of religious bloodshed which defiled our Statute-book"—the heretic was to be burned on a high place before the people.

William Sautre, a parish priest at Lynn, was the first victim at St. Paul's Cross in March, 1402, and nine years later a layman, John Badby, was committed to the flames in the presence of the Prince of Wales for a denial of transubstantiation. The Act was repealed in 1533, but revived in 1559, by Henry the Eighth, as a penalty for denying transubstantiation (the doctrine of the living Presence in the consecrated bread).

A number of persons were burnt to death in Henry's reign, some as Protestants, and some as Roman Catholics, but in the reign of his daughter Mary (which, it will be remembered, lasted only six years), nearly three hundred Protestants were committed to the flames—an Archbishop, Bishops, clergymen and laymen; rich and poor, men, women and even some half dozen children, figured in this ghastly outbreak of religious intolerance. Sufferers were sent in batches to the flames. In a single day, 13 victims, two of them women, were burnt at Stratford-le-Bow. Such was the work of the evil, soured woman who will always be known by the name of "Bloody Mary."

It was the practice for centuries to sentence women found guilty of treason, or petty treason (murder of husband or master, or the head of a religious house) to death by burning, while men found guilty of these offences were hanged, drawn and quartered. This distinction, it is interesting to note, was not on grounds of mercy, but of decency, burning being considered "more decent than hanging, disembowelling, and exposure on a gibbet."

The sentence of death by burning, passed by the infamous Jeffreys upon Dame Alice Lisle, at the commencement of the Bloody Assize, was probably a legal one, but the method of the so-called trial, and the weakness of the case upon which the jury were brow-beaten to return a verdict of guilty; the saintly character of the doomed woman, and her advanced years, have made the case one of the most terrible of that frightful Assize. That she did not endure the sentence of burning, but was beheaded, was not due to any change in Jeffreys' evil purpose, which was to kill her by any means possible.

Another unfortunate victim of Jeffreys, Elizabeth Gaunt, a young married woman, was actually burned to death, upon a conviction for treason. This woman was betrayed by the man Burton, to whom she had given shelter, and whose life she had saved, and, although she had done a great work amongst the unfortunate women in the London prisons, and was of blameless life, she could not be saved.

She was dragged on a hurdle to Tyburn, and there burnt at the stake. She was literally burned alive, as the Judges had ordered, the mercy of being first strangled having been refused her.

Penn, the great Quaker, "saw the executioners thrust their torches into the sheaves and noted that she met a horrible death with calmness and dignity, arranging the straw about her feet that the flames might do their work more quickly . . . When the huge crowd stood around saw this foul deed, many wept aloud and uttered lamentation and prayers for their murdered country-woman."

The last woman burnt in Scotland appears to have been a woman accused of being a witch in 1708, but burnings went on in England for 80 years after this date, the last recorded case taking place in 1789.

Before the abolition of this cruel form of death, the practice had grown up of strangling the doomed woman before her body was burnt. This was the sentence passed on one of two women convicted of murder at Horsham, Sussex, in July, 1752. Sarah Pledge (a married woman with seven children) and her cousin, Anne Whale, murdered James Whale, the husband of the latter woman by administering poison. Pledge was sentenced to death by hanging. It is recorded that she was accompanied to the place of execution by one of her children, and that, on seeing the hangman, Jack Ketch, she openly stated her aversion to him, and told him she would rather go naked to the gallows than that he should have her clothes. "But;" says the chronicler, "Jack Ketch soon deprived her of life, and her clothes."

The woman Whale was led to the stake, where she was chained to the post and then strangled. In five minutes a fire was kindled, and her body burned to ashes.

The last recorded burning of a woman in Yorkshire followed the sentence, passed at York Castle, on March 9th, 1776, upon "Elizabeth, late wife of John Boardingham, guilty of petty treason" (probably the murder of her husband). She was sentenced "to be drawn to the place of execution upon a hurdle, on Wednesday next—to be burned with fire, until dead."

In May, 1777, a girl of just over 14 years of age, was convicted of treason, and was sentenced to be burnt. Apparently her employer had painted, or whitewashed, some farthings to make them appear to be shillings, and the child, at the employer's command, had secreted them. However, they were found, and she, and the man, stood their trial. He was sentenced to be hanged (this was the penalty for coining) and the sentence had already been carried out in his case, and the girl was bound to the stake and the faggots about to be ignited, when Lord Weymouth happened to pass that way, and intervened, with the result that the child's life was ultimately saved.

Commenting upon this frightful sentence passed upon a mere child, the "Quarterly Review" said: "A mere accident saved the nation from this crime, and this national disgrace."

Death by burning was finally abolished in 1790.

CHAPTER XVIII.

TORTURE

The English common law never recognised the legality of torture, with the possible exception of the ordeal of early Norman days, and the brutal punishment of pressing to death. The ordeal was not ordered as a means of inflicting pain, but as a crude and often painful test of innocence or guilt. The peine forte et dure, again, gradually came into legal recognition owing to the difficulty of dealing with a prisoner who refused to plead, and was directed to making him commence the proceedings of the Court by entering a plea, and not with a view to making him confess his crime.

The Bill of Rights (1689) in asserting to William and Mary the "ancient rights and liberties of the people," which had been so often denied to them by the Stuart Kings, clearly laid down, as one of those ancient rights, that cruel and unjust punishments should not be inflicted. When, upon the assassination of George Villiers, Duke of Buckingham, in the reign of Charles I. (1628) it was proposed to put the assassin to the rack, to discover whether he had any accomplices, the Judges, being consulted, declared unanimously that no such torture was allowable by the laws of England. The words of their memorable judgment were "that he ought not, by the law, to be tortured by the rack, for no such punishment is known or allowed by our law." That the words of the judgment recognized the existence of the rack in England at that time as an instrument of torture, is, of course, obvious, and there is no doubt that it had been known and, unfortunately, used, for very many years before.

The Judges must have known. for instance, of the fate of Guido Fawkes (1605) put to the rack, and so severely injured, in the attempt to obtain from him the names of his confederates in the Gunpowder Plot, that he had to be carried to the scaffold for execution.

Cases of the use of torture by the rack occurred so early as the thirteenth century. In Edward IV.'s reign it was in use, and there is a well-established case in 1468. It never became part of the procedure of the ordinary courts, but a free use of the rack was made by great statesmen, and it eventually became one of our political institutions. "The judicial iniquities of Edward IV.'s reign became evil precedents for his successors."

The statement has been made that the rack was introduced into England by the Duke of Exeter, in the reign of Henry VI. (1422-1461), and that it was known as "the Duke of Exeter's daughter," but this may date its more general use.

In the religious disturbances of following reigns it was used considerably, and it seems certain that it played an evil part in criminal procedure for a long time by the order of the Crown, or of some extraordinary tribunal such as the Star Chamber. This sinister Court, which existed from the reign of Henry VII. until it was abolished by the Puritans, became a terrible instrument of cruelty in the hands of unscrupulous kings, for it was peculiarly their own tribunal. It was this Court, which, in 1630, ordered Dr. Leighton, a clergyman, to be pilloried, flogged and deprived of his ears, for writing against the bishops. The same Court, in 1634, passed the dreadful sentence upon Prynne, the lawyer, and again tortured him, with others in 1637. It undoubtedly used the rack, the thumb-screw, and other instruments of torture freely, cruelly, and illegally. Harrison Ainsworth's book, "The Star Chamber," gives a gruesome picture of its activities. Guido Fawkes was racked after his examination by this Court.

During the reigns of Henry VIII., Mary and Elizabeth, the rack was in constant use, as a means of extorting confessions. A melancholy proof of the lengths to which even good men may be tempted to go in the heat of religious controversy is the case of Sir Thomas More, the gentle and learned Chancellor of Henry VIII., who actually visited the Tower to see the torture administered to James Bainham, a Protestant gentleman.

The rack was an invention of extreme cruelty, stretching and breaking the tendons, dislocating the joints and reducing the sufferer to complete helplessness and terrible suffering.

It was largely used in the days of the Roman Empire, being legally permitted for the torture of slaves and criminals, and, on the continent, during the religious strife of the Middle Ages, it was constantly employed. It was one of the instruments of torture most freely used by the Inquisition.

Other forms of torture were "the scavenger's daughter," or manacles, which pressed the victim's head to his feet; the "necklace," a spiked collar; and the "thumb-screw," a device for crushing the thumb. These are still to be seen in the Tower of London. A cell, called the "Little Ease," in which the prisoner could neither stand nor lie was another form of cruelty.

In Scotland torture appears to have had more formal recognition than in England, and there are numerous records of its use, in the Register of the Privy Council. Amongst the most celebrated forms used in Scotland was the "boot," a long iron boot, into which the foot was inserted, wedges being then driven between the limb and the boot, crushing the leg, and inflicting acute agony. It was probably introduced from the Continent, where there are records of its use in criminal trials. In 1605, a suit was brought against the Earl of Orkney, for putting a son of one of his enemies to this torture, and it was undoubtedly used by great noblemen for their own ends.

How much torture was used by gaolers in the evil English prisons of other days will never be known. It is recorded that, in the wild anarchy of Stephen's reign (1135-1154) fiendish tortures were inflicted upon hapless prisoners confined by the turbulent barons in their own castles. Centuries afterwards, in the eighteenth century, the torture of helpless prisoners was still being carried on, for a committee which sat in the reign of George I. reported that the gaolers were taking upon themselves magisterial duties, and imposing fines after commitment, and fearful castigations for those who revolted. It was found that thumb-screws and leg-shears were used at the will of the keeper, and that iron collars were tightened until blood issued from eyes, nose, and ears, and that instruments of torture were kept in the London prisons and much used.

CHAPTER XIX

PEINE FORTE ET DURE

("The strong and hard pain," or Pressing to Death)

In the long list of cruel punishments of other days, none was so revolting in its execution and its motive as the peine forte et dure. How long it was in use in the administration of English law is not known, but cases are to be found so early as the reign of Edward I. (1272-1307).

"But what if the suspect would not put himself upon his country? It is clear that for a long time after 1215 the law did not know what to do with him. The abolition of the ordeal had disturbed all its arrangements. We take it that, under the old procedure a man who refused to go to the ordeal to which he had been sent might be put to death, though perhaps rather as an ordeal than as a convict—he had renounced the law declared by the Court . . . In 1219, when the first eyre (circuit of the Judges) of Henry III.'s reign was in progress, the King's Council was compelled to meet the needs of the moment by instructions sent to the Judges . . . Not one word was said about compelling people to abide a trial, or of trying by jury men who had not put themselves upon the country. All details were expressly left to the discretion of the Judges.

"On the rolls of the last years of Henry III.'s reign we see all the suspects putting themselves upon the country with an exemplary regularity which can only be the result of some powerful motive. In 1275, Edward I. found it necessary to declare that notorious felons who were openly of ill-fame and would not put themselves upon inquests should be kept in strong and hard prison . . . Soon afterwards we learn that their imprisonment is to be of the most rigorous kind. They are ironed; they lie on the ground in the prison's worst place; they have a little bread one day, a little water the next.

A few years later we hear that the prisoner is to be laden with as much iron as he can bear, and thus in course of time the hideous peine forte et dure was developed."

(Pollock & Maitland's "History of English Law.")

Why, it may be asked, was so much emphasis laid upon the necessity for compelling a prisoner to plead? The torture followed a sentence, imposed by a Judge of Assize, upon an accused person who had not yet been found guilty, and was used for the specific and evil purpose of compelling him to plead to the charge, so that, if found guilty, not only would his life be forfeit, but his unfortunate relatives and dependents would be deprived of his estate. Standing mute at a trial "was not held equivalent to guilt or confession until 1772 when the statute law intervened" (says Lord Birkenhead in "Famous Trials") "and then only to declare that a man who refused to plead should be taken to be convicted. It was not until 1827, little over 100 years ago, that the sensible rule was adopted that a deliberate refusal to plead was not an admission to guilt, and that

THE FORDWICH DUCKING STOOL

125

NEWBURY STOCKS

consequently the real solution was to proceed with the trial in order to ascertain whether the prisoner was guilty or not.

"It may be asked" (he continues), "why should a prisoner give all this trouble?" There was, of course, a serious reason. In those days conviction for felony entailed forfeiture and corruption of blood. Conviction meant, as a rule, a lingering and painful death, as hanging then was. Pressing to death was worse, but not too markedly more painful. A prisoner who was without hope of acquittal or reprieve knew that by his condemnation, not only was his life forfeit, but his wife and family were beggared and deprived of all hope of assistance from others. If, therefore, he could steel himself to be pressed to death, then he could die unconvicted."

The unfortunate person received the sentence in these terrible words:—

"That you be taken back to the prison whence you came to a low dungeon into which no light can enter; that you be laid upon your back on the bare floor with a cloth round your loins but elsewhere naked; that there be set upon your body a weight of iron as great as you can bear, and greater. That you have no sustenance save on the first day three morsels of the coarsest bread; on the second day three draughts of stagnant water; on the third day bread as before; next day water as before; until you die."

The object of this protracted torture, inflicted upon a prisoner not yet tried and convicted, was to allow him, at any stage in the torture to plead, and thus to allow the law to take its ordinary course. "Later, when the practice of pressing to death was almost obsolete, prisoners who declined to plead were tortured, in order to compel them to do so, by twisting and screwing their thumbs with whipcord. In 1721, a woman, Mary Andrews, was subjected to this punishment. After bearing with fortitude the first three whipcords, which broke from the violence of the twisting, she submitted to plead at the fourth."

(William Andrews in "Bygone Punishments.")

The Press Room at Newgate took its name from the punishment of pressing to death, such sentences being carried out in this cell. There it was that Major George Strangeways, a distinguished soldier of the Civil War, refusing to plead to a charge of murder, was pressed to death in February 1658. A square wooden frame was placed upon his body, and iron weights placed upon it. The pain was terrible, but it seemed that he might live for a long time, so his friends hastened his death, at his request, by standing on the frame, and after a few minutes of dreadful pain, he succumbed.

Many of those who received the sentence found that their endurance was not equal to the ordeal, and, often terribly injured, were carried back to Court to face their trial.

J. Horsfall Turner, in "Wakefield Prison," refers to the case of Calverley, a Yorkshireman who was pressed to death at York Castle in 1605.

"His family had been lords of Calverley many generations before the Stuarts came to England. The Calverley parish register, under date April 24th, 1605, contains the bare entry, 'Willm and Walter, sonns of Walter Calverley, Esquire,' amongst the burials. They were the victims of what was still called the Calverley murder, on which was founded a play called "A Yorkshire Tragedy," ascribed by some to Shakespeare, and included in his collected works in one or two editions. This, however, is certainly an error, as anyone may percieve who examines the style and language used.

"In an insane moment, maddened by drinking, gambling, and jealousy, and fancying that his children would be brought to beggary by his dissipated habits, he killed his two sons as recorded, attempted to kill his wife at Calverley Hall (now converted into cottage tenements) and rode off to murder his boy Henry, who was placed out to be nursed, but being overtaken and captured, he was examined before Sir John Savile and Sir Thomas Bland, on the 24th April 1605 (the same day as the funeral of the boys, and the day after the murders) who sent him temporarily to Wakefield.

"Soon afterwards he was conveyed to York Castle, where he was found guilty and sentenced to death. Such a doom would never be entertained now, for it was certainly a case of insanity.

"Having come to his senses he refused to plead (and in so doing proved his return to sanity) in order to save his goods and estate for his only remaining son, Henry, who lived to enjoy them.

"He was therefore, called to endure the 'peine forte et dure,' that is, being pressed to death.

"The burial register at St. Mary's Castlegate, York, has the entry of his interment, 'Walter Calverley, executed for murdering his own children, the 23rd of April, 1605, was buried on the 10 August, 1605.' A tradition was held at Calverley that, after a pretended burial at York, his remains were conveyed to Calverley for interment. Down to the present generation the natives of Calverley have believed that the ghost of the mudered man rides a fleeting headless horse around the estate. Boys used to have a saying, 'A pund of more weight, lig on, lig on,' in remembrance of the distressing request of Calverley to be crushed to death more speedily."

The inscription on the tomb at York is, technically, incorrect, for Calverley was not "executed for murdering his children," but lost his life by refusing to plead, so that he was never found legally guilty of the murders. J. Horsfall Turner, it will be noticed, refers to him as "the murdered man," and possibly he is correct. Although the sentence of the Court contained the words "until you die," there was no law which legalised such a death. The law did not deal with the position of a man who refused to plead, and the custom grew up of attempting to make men plead by this inhuman method.

Note from "The Hangman's Record." February 28th, 1723:—
"William Spiggot and Thomas Phillips for highway robbery, executed at Tyburn. These two convicts were put to the torture in the Press Yard for refusing to plead.

CHAPTER XX.

THE BRANDING IRON

For centuries the branding of criminals was a common form of punishment in England, but there are records of its use long before the Saxons brought the custom to this country. Branding, for instance, was a punishment sanctioned by the Babylonian law possibly 4,000 years before Christ. It was inflicted for slander on a married woman or a priestess. Greek slaves were branded by their owners, and the Romans used it for identification of slaves and gladiators, and for punishment.

The punishment was adopted by the Anglo-Saxons and continued by the Normans, and many old statutes authorised the burning of descriptive letters on the face or body. The robber was branded with the letter "R," and the blasphemer with the letter "B." The letters "S.L." signified a seditious libeller. Perhaps the most tragic record in English history with regard to branding is that Englishmen could be branded with the letter "S," signifying slave. An Act passed in the reign of the youthful King Edward VI. (probably at the instigation of the Protector, Somerset), against the unfortunate vagrants who were the victims of so many statutes, laid down that any idle and vagabond person, taken before a Justice should (the sentence was imperative and not optional) be branded in the breast with the letter "V," and then followed the almost unbelievable sentence— "He shall be adjudged *to be a slave to the person presenting him* for two years; to be fed with bread and water, and be put to work, however vile soever it be, by beating, chaining, etc.: and if he runs away, the Justice, on conviction, shall cause such slave to be marked on the forehead or the ball of the cheek, with the sign of an 'S,' and shall further adjudge him to be his master's slave for ever, and if he again run away, he shall suffer death as a felon." (1547)

The informer, therefore, if he could satisfy the Justice that the poor fellow was an idle person and a vagabond, received him, by the sentence of the Justice, as his slave for two years. If, by his cruelty, condoned by the law in the form of beating or chaining, he drove the unfortunate wretch to despair and to flight, he could secure him as his slave for ever.

There is no record of how many persons suffered under this inhuman law, and it was repealed in 1636. Under the same statute gypsies could be branded as vagrants, and those who created a disturbance in a Church were branded with the letter "F" (fray-maker).

Before the Act was repealed, it was laid down that rogues, vagabonds and sturdy beggars, were to be committed to the common gaol, and, if convicted at the next Quarter Sessions or Assizes, to be "grievously whipped, and burnt through the gristle of the right ear with a hot iron of the compass of an inch about," so that it would appear that the earlier statute had not greatly reduced the numbers of the vagrants. Possibly its brutality made some Justices reluctant to use the powers given to them.

Cruelty to the vagabond became such an ordinary matter that in the first year of James I. (1603) all men whatever their station, were ordered to apprehend such rogues or vagabonds as they might see begging; to convey them to the nearest constable or tything-man, who (apparently without trial) was empowered to brand them with the letter "R" (rogue).

The gypsies were pursued with the same savage cruelty. William Andrews gives an instance at Haddington, in 1636, in which gypsies were horribly treated, the men being hanged, the women drowned (with the exception of those who had children), the latter being scourged through the burgh and burnt on their cheeks.

In 1656, James Naylor, of Ardsley, a Quaker preacher, suffered a dreadful sentence. He had served in the Parliamentary Army with distinction; came under the influence of George Fox and became a powerful preacher of the Society of Friends. Under the influence of intense religious enthusiasm, he committed the indiscretion of allowing some foolish people at Bristol to worship him, and to lead him in procession into the town on horseback, singing as they went, in imitation of the way in which Christ entered Jerusalem. He was seized and imprisoned, and the sentence passed upon him included standing in the pillory; being publicly whipped, both in London and Bristol; having his tongue bored through with a hot iron, and finally to be imprisoned with hard labour till released by Parliament. Many petitions were signed on his behalf, but the whole sentence was carried through, Naylor bearing it all most patiently. He was kept in prison for some years. He fully repented and made confession of his sin, and was forgiven and received back by the Friends. His last words, two hours before his death, were, "There is a spirit that I feel, that delights to do no evil, nor to revenge any wrong, but delights to endure all things." He had, in truth, endured all things.

From the reign of Henry VII. branding was inflicted for all offences which involved benefit of clergy and this remained the law until 1822. In 1698 it was enacted that those convicted of petty thefts, who were entitled to benefit of clergy, should be burnt "in the most visible part of the left cheek, nearest the nose," but this was repealed 11 years later.

When the sentence was one of branding on the hand, the hand was placed in a "hold-fast" and the appropriate letter was then burnt into the thick part of the thumb with the red-hot iron. The photograph on page 147 was very kindly supplied by the curator of Lancaster Castle, and it shews a branding iron (on the right) fastened vertically to the wall of the Assize Court there, and a hand bearing the branded letter "M" (for malefactor). Needless to say, the letter is reproduced in ink, and is not an actual branding. The sentence was, it would appear, carried out in open Court. The warder entered with the red-hot iron, and pressed it against the criminal's thumb. Then he would look up to the Judge and cry, "A fair mark, my Lord?" If the Judge nodded, the criminal was released; if not, the branding had to be repeated, an agonising ordeal for the prisoner. The last record of this iron being used is dated 1811.

It was the practice at Assizes and Quarter Sessions to order prisoners to hold up their hands before passing sentence— prisoners carried their own records of previous convictions in those days.

Branding was quite an ordinary sentence at the Courts of Quarter Sessions and Assizes.

At the Assizes held at York on March 9th, 1776, no less than eight prisoners were ordered to be branded as a part of their sentences, six men and two women, all suffering terms of imprisonment varying between six months and one year, in addition to the branding.

In the eighteenth century prisoners of higher rank managed, by some means, to influence the Courts so that their sentences were branding with a cold iron. In 1782 a clergyman killed a man in a duel in Hyde Park; he was found guilty of manslaughter and escaped with a sentence of branding with a cold iron. Sentences of this kind, and their marked distinction between prisoners of different stations in life, led to the practice of branding becoming obsolete. It was finally abolished in 1829, except in the case of deserters in the army, and the practice, after that year, was to tattoo defaulting soldiers with ink or gunpowder.

CHAPTER XXI.

THE SCOLD'S BRIDLE OR BRANK

For more than two centuries—the seventeenth, the eighteenth, and half of the nineteenth—the instrument known as the "Scold's Bridle" or "Brank" was used almost exclusively for the punishment of women. It took many forms, but the principle was always the same—a metal cage securing the head, so that a piece of metal should enter the mouth, pressing down and securing the tongue and thus effectually gagging the woman. Generally the projection was smooth, but there are some of these instruments still in existence which prove that occasionally, the projection was either spiked or roughened, to ensure greater pain.

The scold was always a very unpopular member of the community. The definition of such a woman:—

"A troublesome and angry woman, who by brawling and wrangling amongst her neighbours, breaks the public peace, increases discord, and becomes a public nuisance to the neighbourhood" is not a description of a pleasant type of person. Her type still exists, but on the other hand, there are many men to-day to whom the description would equally apply, and, looking back from the twentieth century, it is hard to understand now why women were singled out for a punishment which was never a legal one, and always a cruel one, whilst unneighbourly quarrelsome and malicious men went free.

In view of this inequality and injustice, it is pleasant to recall that one strong-minded Yorkshire Justice, in 1770 (the incident is recorded in the chapter on the pillory) having heard the complaint of the husband who took his wife to him as a common scold, and having heard the woman's version of the facts, decided that he would have the pair ducked, a sentence which was duly carried out. No statute ever authorised the use of this brutal instrument, and its origin is doubtful. It is certain that it was used in Scotland long before anyone in authority ventured to order its use in England, so that the inference appears to be a fair one—either that Scotsmen were more cruel than Englishmen, or had less endurance and patience, or that Scotswomen were more virulent in tongue than Englishwomen! It was used in Edinburgh in 1567, and at Glasgow in 1574, but it was in the seventeenth century that it made its appearance in England. Although scolds are frequently mentioned in the proceedings before the West Riding Quarter Sessions, there is no record of one ever having been sentenced to the punishment of the bridle, or brank. A rather unusual sentence was passed upon a scold at the Wakefield Sessions on October 4th, 1614:-

"Scold. Whereas Ann Walker, daughter of John Walker, of Slaughthwaite, did in the time of ye sessions heare holden, in ye open streets, call one Andrew Shaw 'cuckoe,' for prosecuting a bill of indictment on ye King's behalfe against her father. Ordered. That the constable of Wakefield shall cause ye said Ann Walker, for her impudent and bold behaviour, to be runge through ye town of Wakefield with basins before her, as is accustomed for common scoldes."

The offence seems to have been a very slight one, and, although the sentence of the Court speaks of the custom for common scolds, the sentence was an extraordinary one.

Usually the punishment for scolds was the ducking-stool, or exposure in the cucking-stool or at the market cross. In some cases the offence was dealt with as a breach of the peace only, and the offender was ordered to find sureties for good behaviour.

There is a record in the minutes of the Macclesfield Corporation of the use of the brank in 1623. This appears to be the earliest date as far as is known. The Walton-on-Thames brank (mentioned below) is dated 1632, so that it seems a fair assumption that the instrument was in use, probably, in other places by that date. Later there are records which shew that it was used not only by the Justices, but by corporations and lords of manors, who had assumed the authority to use it. A statement, quoted by William Andrews (from a paper read before the Architectural Archaelogical and Historic Society of Chester, published in 1858) gives an extraordinary story of the way in which the Congleton brank was used:—

"It was formerly in the hands of the town gaoler, whose services were not infrequently called into requisition. In the old-fashioned, half-timbered houses in the borough, there was generally fixed on one side of the large open fireplaces a hook, so that when a man's wife indulged her scolding propensities, the husband sent for the town gaoler to bring the bridle, and had her bridled and chained to the hook until she promised to behave herself better for the future. I have seen one of these hooks, and have often heard husbands say to their wives: 'If you don't rest with your tongue I'll send for the bridle and hook you up.'

"The Mayor and Justices frequently brought the instrument into use, for when women were brought before them charged with street-brawling, and insulting the constables and others while in the discharge of their duty, they have ordered them to be bridled and led through the borough by the gaoler. The last time this bridle was publicly used was in 1824, when Ann Runcorn was brought before the Mayor charged with scolding and using harsh language to the constables and churchwardens as they went, on the Sunday morning, round the town to see that all the public-houses were empty and closed during divine service."

The official deputed to lead the woman through the town on this last occasion was the "Magistrates' clerk's clerk!" She appears to have been actually led by the "town clerk's clerk." Possibly the Magistrate's clerk's assistant, who was not under the authority of the Mayor, as such, raised some objection to taking part in a procession in which, the story relates, "hundreds of the inhabitants" took part.

The brank at Bolton-le-Moore, Lancashire, is stated to have been used so late as 1856.

The illustration shews the scold's bridle in the Church at Walton-on-Thames. It is of a very simple form, the two iron bands passing over the head from front to back, round the face, and then being secured by a padlock at the back. The junction at the back, towards the top of the head, seems to indicate that there was a slot, and a nut and hole, which enabled the band over the head to be tightened up or expanded.

The tradition associated with this bridle is that it was a gift to the parish from a man named Chester, who had suffered greatly from a woman's lying tongue. It bears the date 1632, and the following inscription:—

"Chester presents Walton with a bridle
To curb women's tongues that talk too idle."

With the instrument on her head, the unhappy woman was led through the streets of the town, and exposed to the jeers and insults of the crowd, an object of contempt. The sentence could be imposed by the local Justices, and it is to be feared that it was used not only as a punishment for those whose malicious tongues had brought them before the Justices, but also, on occasion, against women who had only denounced evil, and the evil-doer. On other occasions it seems to have been used as a gag for women sentenced to be ducked, a cruel addition to a terrible sentence.

Mr. William Andrews, in "Bygone Punishments," gives one case in which the brank was used upon a man, one James Brodie, a blind beggar, who murdered a boy, who was his guide, in Nottingham Forest, in 1799. During his imprisonment, prior to his execution, the murderer was so noisy that the brank was used to keep him quiet until his execution.

In 1821 this brank was still kept in readiness at Nottingham Castle, and a Judge of Assize ordered that it should be destroyed.

The Ipswich bridle is dated 1675, and an old record of the town seems to suggest that the culprit was driven through the streets there in a cart, or fastened in a chair, which was known as the "gogging" or "gagging" chair, or "Tewe," as a public warning and humiliation.

An extract from the Ipswich Domesday Book runs thus: "Woman that bene common chiders, and will not chastise their ill tongue to myssaye (mis-say) folk, let them be chastised by the justice called ye 'Tewe' or else let them make grievous ransome if they have wharof (whereof)."

The significance of this quotation lies in the fact that, at Ipswich, there appears to have been a practice of gagging scolds as they were wheeled through the town; in other words, a very early form of brank, or bridle, dating back to the earliest years of the Normans.

CHAPTER XXII.

BODY IRONS

The use of body-irons upon all offenders, whether convicted, or awaiting trial, was general until well into the eighteenth century.

The famous prison reformer, John Howard, writing of the County Gaol at Hereford (probably between 1773 and 1775) said: "Convicts were generally robust young men who had been accustomed to free diet, tolerable lodgings, and vigorous exercise. On entering prison they were ironed; thrust into close offensive dungeons, some of them without straw or bedding, and remained two-thirds of the 24 hours utterly inactive. Ely Gaol (the letter continued) was the property of the Bishop, and because of the insecurity of the old prison (rebuilt about 1763) the gaoler chained the victims down on their backs on the floor, across which were several iron bars, with an iron collar with spikes about their necks, and a heavy iron bar over their legs. Mr. James Collyer, J.P., reported the matter to the King, who gave immediate orders for a proper enquiry and redress."

A minute of West Riding Quarter Sessions of April 30th, 1728, recorded that it was agreed, respecting York Castle Gaol that as many prisoners had died of mortification of the limbs, an apothecary should be appointed to attend to the prisoners.

High up on the wall of the old Fire Station at Doncaster, in a bricked-up window, are still hanging the set of body-irons shewn in the illustration.

A collar for the neck, the large ring for the waist, and the two small rings for the ankles, all connected by the heavy links of the chains—the weight alone of these irons must have been a trying burden to the unfortunate prisoner, and, as, if he were a tall man, it would be impossible to stand upright in them, the suffering must have been considerable. Amongst the many intolerable injustices of prison life in the eighteenth century was that of charging the prisoner a fee for the use of these irons. On the State side of Newgate Prison, the prisoner was charged three guineas for admission; for light irons, one guinea; for rent of bed, half a guinea a week, and for another guinea he could have coals and candles, plates and a knife. On the Master's side the admission fee was thirteen shillings and sixpence, irons half a guinea; rent of a bed, or part of a bed, half a crown, and such food as ordered and paid for. If the prisoner was too poor to pay anything he escaped these dues, but endured instead the unspeakable squalor, exposure and hunger of the common side of the prison.

Albert Crew in his book, "The Old Bailey," says: "Premiums from £20 to £500 were demanded and the prisoner had to decide between submitting to this extortion or taking up his abode in the common side, where he had thieves and villains for his associates, and was, in the words of an inmate, 'perpetually tormented and eaten by vermin.' The weight of chains again depended upon the price a prisoner could pay for 'easement of irons,' and it was a common practice to overload a newcomer with enormous fetters, and so terrify him into disbursement.

For those unable to purchase the squalid comforts of the Master's side was reserved the common side, which was mainly composed of underground dungeons, into which the prisoners were lowered, to fight with rats for the meagre pittance of food thrown to them."

In 1690, John Bernardi, arrested for political reasons, was thrown into Newgate, and, in his own words, "loaded with heavy irons, and put into a dark stinking apartment."

He was kept in custody for 12 months by a special Act, and, by successive Acts, he was kept a prisoner, without a charge being made against him, until he died in 1736, still untried, after nearly 50 years' imprisonment. He married whilst in Newgate, and his devoted wife voluntarily stayed with him in his captivity, no less than ten children being born to them within the precincts of the prison. Charles Dickens (in "Barnaby Rudge") has given a description of Barnaby's reception at Newgate Prison after his capture by the soldiers, and after he had been taken before Sir John Fielding at Bow Street: "A smith was speedily in attendance, who rivetted upon him a set of heavy irons. Stumbling on as well as he could beneath the unusual burden of these fetters, he was conducted to a strong stone cell, where, fastening the door with locks and bolts and chains, they left him well secured; having first, unseen by him, thrust in Grip, who with his head drooping, and his deep black plumes rough and rumpled, appeared to comprehend and to partake his master's fallen fortunes."

The set of irons rivetted upon Barnaby Rudge were, in all probability, exactly similar to those still to be seen at Doncaster. Once they had been secured upon the prisoner only the smith could remove them, unless the prisoner and his friends, if he escaped, could file them through, or knock them off with a hammer. When Newgate Gaol was stormed by the mob during the Gordon riots of 1780, the 300 prisoners released were hurriedly supplied with tools to enable them to remove their irons, and Dickens describes how Barnaby, "heavily ironed as he was . . . knelt down in a corner of the market, among the pens for cattle, and knocked off his father's irons, and then when he had seen him spring, a free man, to his feet, he went to work upon his own, which soon fell rattling to the ground, and left his limbs unfettered.

"Gliding away together when this task was accomplished and passing several groups of men, each gathered round a stooping figure to hide him from those who passed, but unable to repress the clanking sound of the hammers, which told that they, too, were busy with the same work—the two fugitives made towards Clerkenwell, and passing thence to Islington, were quickly in the fields."

Apparently the hammers were used to knock out the rivets which held the iron rings fast round the neck, waist and ankles; they would have been useless for breaking the solid rings.

CHAPTER XXIII.

PUNISHMENTS IN A YORKSHIRE TOWN

Although the available records are scanty, it is possible to obtain sufficient evidence to prove that Yorkshire had a considerable number of local gaols, apart from the main prison at York Castle, and (later) Wakefield House of Correction. Amongst these there was for centuries a Doncaster "Jail," its history commencing with the West Bar, "a praty Tower of stone," noted by John Leland (1506-1552), on his antiquarian tour through England between 1536 and 1542, as still standing.

A Noncomformist minister named Fisher, of Sheffield, was imprisoned in several Yorkshire prisons, including Doncaster, about the year 1662, and in the West Riding Sessions Rolls it is recorded that, at Pontefract, in April 1687, "Doncaster, having its own gaol, is free from paying moneys to York Castle." At some later date a dispute began between Doncaster Corporation and the Wakefield Prison authorities as to payments claimed by the prison, for, on October 7th, 1725, at the West Riding Sessions, it was ordered that prisoners committed to Wakefield from Leeds, Doncaster, Pontefract, and the Honour of Halifax, should not be received in future. Apparently Wakefield Prison speedily repented of this attitude of aloofness, for, three years later, the order was rescinded, and a new order made against the four towns to pay their share of repairs to the prison and the master's salary.

In 1767 a new "goal" (the old way of spelling "gaol" was built at Doncaster, to which, in 1773, a temporary infirmary was ordered to be added. While Doncaster was going ahead, Wakefield Prison had, it would seem, deteriorated, for in 1775, a letter from John Howard to Wakefield Sessions was sent on to be considercd at the Doncaster Sessions. Possibly this implies that Wakefield felt that Doncaster should bear some blame for John Howard's criticisms, because of their refusal to share in the costs of the larger prison.

The 1767 prison at Doncaster must have been a very small building. The account (for labour only) runs thus: "Received 26th September, 1769, of the Corporation of Doncaster the sum of £81/3/6, being in full for building and completing their New Gaol by me, according to agreement, JOHN MOSLEY." It must have been as unsatisfactory as it was small, for ten years later it was taken down and a new one erected, but, before this was carried out, John Howard visited the town and the gaol, and his brief report is as follows:—

Doncaster Town Gaol.

Two rooms for felons, and two over them for debtors. All have chimneys. No water. Keeper, one of the sergeants-at-mace, lives distant. Fees 1/4. Allowance to felons 4d. per day.

Possibly the comment that the gaoler lived away from the gaol is reflected in an order of the Corporation of January 22nd, 1783, that "a house be erected for the under gaoler to live in, in the courtyard, for the greater security of the safe keeping of the prisoners." Up to this time the gaoler had always lived away from the prison. At one period (about 1728) the gaoler was a woman, one Elizabeth Lee, the widow of the previous gaoler, for, on September 29th in that year she appeared in Court and made a return of all the prisoners then confined.

The gaol, erected in 1779, is described by another visitor thus: "This gaol is a detached building in St. Sepulchre Gate. The keeper's house overlooks the Court . . . For all kinds of prisoners one small flagged court, with a pump. Felons have two good-sized rooms below; one totally dark, except a small aperture in the door; the other has an iron-grated window, not glazed. Above stairs are two rooms with iron-grated and glazed windows, for debtors. The rooms have fireplaces. The borough allows fuel in winter, straw on bedsteads, two blankets and a rug. Debtors are brought here by process on Borough writs to any amount; likewise for smaller sums from the Court of Requests. No sewer, nor means for decent cleanliness; the prison most intolerably offensive. The gaoler told me it was usually so."

Then follows a statement that the gaoler was a man of slx feet three inches; his weight 39 stones eight pounds; and (a significant comment) "much feared on account of his grip."

In 1802 the allowance to debtors and felons was 4d. or 6d. per day "as bread was cheap or dear."

A long controversy appears to have been carried on with regard to this gaol between the West Riding Justices, in Quarter Sessions, and the Corporation, but, during this period the gaol was visited by the famous Quaker prison reformer Elizabeth Fry, with her brother, Mr. J. J. Gurney, also a Quaker, and their report, under date August 20th, 1818, has been preserved and gives much light upon the conditions in this and other local prisons: -

"This gaol consists of a small courtyard, two rooms on the ground floor, and two others above them; the rooms severally furnished with a small bed and measuring 13 feet square.

"Of the lower rooms, one is for male criminals of all descriptions, and the other for male vagrants. Of the upper rooms one is for females, whether debtors, vagrants, or criminals; the other for male debtors.

"Fifteen persons have at times been locked up together for the night in the apartment allotted to male criminals, that apartment measuring, as before stated 13 feet square. The state of these poor wretches, when thus situated, must have been in a very high degree miserable and unhealthy.

"In the male vagrants' room there is no light when the door is shut, except through a hole in the door, and, of course, no ventilation. The criminals in this gaol are ironed. They are allowed 8d. per day, and firing, but neither clothing nor soap. They are totally unemployed and receive no instruction whatever.

"Forty persons have been confined in this gaol at once. At this time there were only five prisoners there.

"The doors of the four rooms being necessarily kept open during the day, the prisoners of all descriptions, debtors and criminals, males and females associate freely together. Who can wonder that crimes increase? Who does not perceive the tendency of such an association to convert into felons the vagrants the misdemeanant and the debtor. One of the vagrants at this time in the prison was a Scotch woman, who, having lost her husband, and having herself just recovered from a serious illness, was travelling homeward in company with her little girl. She complained bitterly of the situation. 'What could I do?' she said, 'I dare not steal; I liked not to beg; destitute and afflicted, what could I do but apply to the magistrates for a pass? The consequence is that I am shut up for a week in prison, and exposed to the worst and most vicious of men.'

"The case speaks for itself. We were much gratified that the intelligent magistrates of Doncaster are anxious to correct these lamentable abuses. We are informed of their intention to erect a new prison."

Nothing was done for some years, but in 1828 there was correspondence between the West Riding Justices and the Corporation, upon the condition and deficiences of the prison (the holding of Sessions in Doncaster having been, in the meantime, suspended). The comment of the local historian, Tomlinson, is a pointed one:—

"The Doncaster Borough jail was evidently a type of many such inadequate buildings throughout the country, the impression of municipal bodies being that prisons must not be made too comfortable, or imprisonment would lose its terrors. Thus it was that our Corporation, not being anxious for improvements, consumed the first quarter of the nineteenth century in protestations, promises, and making arrangements how to do it."

The new gaol was at last erected, the total cost being about £3,000, the materials from the old premises being utilised. This was the third gaol erected in the immediate neighbourhood during a period of 60 years, and the illustration on page 118 is of this third prison.

A man named Timms was appointed gaoler, his salary 100 guineas a year, covering this appointment, and that of Chief Constable. (*See note at the end of the chapter.)

By the year 1836, Doncaster appears to have entered into a contract for some prisoners to be taken by Wakefield Prison, and they appear to have chosen an unfortunate time to do so, for the following year they received a demand for their proportion of £3,500 about to be spent upon rebuilding the women's prison there. By 1874 all the borough prisoners were being taken to Wakefield, and in 1874 it was reported that the Doncaster contribution was one of the largest payments made by any Corporation in the Riding.

In August, 1880, the Corporation received a surprise in the shape of a writ from the Government for £2,954/4/- and interest, for Wakefield Prison dues, alleged to be unpaid. The Corporation entered an appearance, but the Government gracefully withdrew!

Such is the typical history of a small Corporation gaol, and its contribution to the miseries and the degradation of prisoners of all kinds.

THE WHIPPING POST

Doncaster, in common with all other towns, had its whipping post. After 1713 this was at the Butter Cross. The Corporation minute reads: "May 5th,

1713—Ordered that a whipping post be set up at the stocks at the Butter Cross for punishing vagrants and sturdy beggars—J. Arthur." But this whipping post must have superseded, or have been in addition to another post, as there are numerous previous records of whippings in Doncaster, for instance:—

"September 8th, 1632. Paid for the beadles for whipping a prisoner, 4d."

"October 27th, 1654. Given to Francis Hoden that was kept in prison all night and whipped for having a false pass, 2d."

In this case the unfortunate Francis appears to have received 2d. from the Borough Chamberlain as a consolation for the thrashing he had received!

There is one case of a woman being whipped twice in a fortnight:—

"1641. Aug. 7th. Paid for whipping Margaret Brompton, of Leeds, 4d."

Fifteen days later, the unfortunate Margaret received a second dose at the hands of the beadle: "Aug. 22nd. Whipping Margaret Brompton another time, 4d."

On December 1st in the same year, the beadles received 1/- for whipping one man and two women. In 1659 the beadle received 4d. for whipping Jane Lightly, and one Robert Ayre (presumably the gaoler), for keeping her in gaol 12 days, 1/8.

The most pathetic entry is the following:—

"Borough Sessions, 30th of March, 1726, before the Recorder, Thomas Rayney (Mayor) and Daniel Whitaker (Alderman and Justice of the Borough) a bill of indictment was found against Elizabeth, the wife of Robert Carr, of Newton, in the Parish of Brampton in the County of Cumberland, labourer, for picking twopence-halfpenny out of the pocket of Margaret Hepworth. Elizabeth Carr pleaded not guilty.

"The traverse jury found her guilty to the value of twopence-halfpenny, and she, being with child, was only ordered to be stripped to the waist by the Common Beadle, to have four lashes, and then to be turned out of the town over the Mill Bridge."

Probably the three worthies who passed this sentence were married men, and fathers of families. It is well that their names should have been perpetuated in connection with this brutal sentence.

At Doncaster, January 28th, 1788, David Rancy was publicly whipped for vagrancy, by order of the West Riding Quarter Sessions.

On the 23rd of May, 1789, Mary Ashforth was tried at the Borough Sessions, found guilty of stealing two pieces of muslin, the property of Mr. Benjamin Earnshaw, and was sentenced to be publicly whipped through the Market on the following Saturday.

She was tied with cords to the tail of a cart, drawn by a horse, and taken from the gaol along St. Sepulchre Gate, Baxter Gate, Market Place, Scot Lane, High Street, and so back to the prison, having received a severe flogging from the under-gaoler.

"Salt and brandy were applied to the lacerated back and shoulders," the record states. It was only two years later that public whippings of women were forbidden, and this must have been one of the last of such degrading exhibitions.

This brief but sad story of an unruly apprentice, is taken from the "Doncaster Gazette" of January 27th, 1834:—

"Mansion House, Doncaster.

"Mr. John Richardson, blacksmith, appeared against Joshua Mitchell, his apprentice, whom he charged with remaining out too late at nights, frequenting houses of ill-fame, and absenting himself sometimes for two and three days together. He said he had been very unruly indeed.

"Committed to Wakefield House of Correction for one, month, and to be flogged."

CUCKING-STOOL AND DUCKING-STOOL

The cucking-stool is mentioned in the accounts of the Chamberlain of Doncaster for the year 1632:—

"April 4th. Paid Mr. Webster for 8 stone 1 lb. of iron for the Cuck-stoole xviis. xid.

"Paid to Edward Mason for making the Cuck-stoole xiis. iiiid.," (but it was probably in existence long before this date).

In 1658 there is an entry of the payment of 6/- for a pole 16 feet long, "to make a cuckstool," but it is likely that, by this time, the cucking-stool had become the ducking-stool, as, during the seventeenth century, the ducking-stool was over the Greyfriars' Pond. It consisted of a long pole, hanging over the dirty water of the pond, wherein the offender, strapped in the chair, was dipped three times, the pole swinging on a pivot on piles driven into the ground near the pond.

"It was also brought into requisition at Friar's Bridge. The scold was conducted along the approach to the Cheswold, from the west side of French Gate. Here the instrument hung by a pulley fastened to a beam about the middle of the bridge and the female having been fixed in it, she was let under water three times successively, and then taken out. The bridge was then of timber, before the present stone one was erected. On the back panel of the ducking-stool was, it is said, an engraving representing devils laying hold of scolds."

(Hatfield's "Historical Notices of Doncaster.")

THE STOCKS

The stocks formerly stood at the Butcher Cross in High Street, but were taken away following a minute of the Corporation dated February 3rd, 1725. They faced the north-east angle of Baxter Gate from High Street.

Previously there were stocks in the Market Place and it would seem that, after those at the Butcher Cross had been taken down, they were re-erected in the Market Place:—

October, 1657. Paid to William Thomlinson for making the stocks in the Market Place, 1/6.

August 17th, 1743. One pair of stocks in Market Place, 18/-.

February 13th, 1768. Mr. John Butler for mending the Market Place stocks, 1/-

The last stocks stood near the Parish Church-yard, "placed behind the pump," in St. George Gate.

THE PILLORY

"The pillory was anciently a post erected on a cross-road by the lord, as a mark of his seignory, with his arms on it. The spot chosen at Doncaster seems to have been after the custom of our ancestors, viz.: at the junction of three roads, High Street, Baxter Gate and French Gate." (Hatfield.)

There appears to have been a pump close to the pillory, called the Pillory Well, and there are frequent entries relating to the pillory and the pump.

A new pillory was set up in 1652, and there is an item for repairs in 1760.

At the time of the publication of Hatfield's "Historical Notices" (1868) an old gamekeeper was still living in Doncaster who remembered the pillory, and could describe it.

THE GALLOWS

In 1574, there is a still grimmer entry, which is given as it stands, though rendered into present-day English:—

"Reckoning of Mr. Burke, of Doncaster. Alderman. Whereof he asketh allowance for the charge of Robert Sharperey, the murderer, as followeth:—

Paid to Richard Egremond for his surgery 5/-

Paid to Thomas Pyckerd for his board I8 days 9/-

Paid for drink every morning when the surgeon did dress him 1/6

For keeping, locking and watching him 1/-

Paid for making the gallows 1/-

Paid to the hangman . . . . 6d.

Paid for half of the irons that the said Sharperey did hang in 2/-

It is evident that, so late as the sixteenth century, the Corporation, as manorial lords, exercised the right of gallows.

Miller, in his chronological table says that the gallows were taken down in the mayoralty of Thomas Coulson, 1614-15, but the removal was only temporary, as the following entries prove: October 4th, 1648.— Paid for the gallas building . . . 8d.

Three labourers for mackinge holes and for carrying wood for the gallas. . . 10d.

Paid for wood for the gallas 7/-

Long before this time Sir Ralph Grey and Sir Robert Wellys were hanged in Doncaster, in 1469.

Sometimes the offender was fortunate enough to meet with mercy. A strange notice appeared in the "Yorkshire Journal" in January, 1789, under the heading "Offence Acknowledged and Pardon Asked."

Two Arksey labourers, John Castle and Richard Harrison, admitted cutting the bank of the river at Bentley, and causing the water to flow out and do considerable damage to the Corn Mill, the property of Sir George Cooke, Bart. "We do therefore," the notice added, "humbly beg pardon of the said Sir George Cooke for having committed the same, and return to him our thanks for his lenity in forbearing to commence a prosecution against us." The men signed the statement with their marks.

The offence was a capital one, and the men would in all probability have been executed had a prosecution been commenced. Did Sir George, as the men could not write, draft the notice, and did he reflect, when doing so, that he was compounding a felony? As he was a Justice of the Peace, a member of a very well-known Doncaster family, he may have decided that, to thus pillory the offenders instead of risking their lives, was a course more in accordance with his own feelings in the matter, and that the risk to himself was negligible.

Note— From the "Doncaster Gazette" of May, 1840.

'The question of making a certain Corporation of the name of Timms look respectable made members of the Town Council at their May meeting scratch their heads.

"One Councillor complained that many respectable inhabitants of the town had said that Mr. Timms looked like a ragged sheep when leading his worship and the Corporation to Church, and that he cut a most sorry figure in his old gown. The Council agreed to Mr. Timms being equipped afresh, 'the new toggery to be provided under the direction of the Committee.'"

CHAPTER XXIV.

TRANSPORTATION

Banishment, as a punishment for political offences was a recognised form of punishment for centuries, and so far back as the reign of Elizabeth, a Vagrancy Act (1597) gave to the Justices in Quarter Sessions the power to banish offenders to places beyond the seas, but it was in the reigns of the Stuarts that transportation first became a real terror to the wrong-doer. James I. ordered a "hundred dissolute persons" to be sent to Virginia in 1619, and in the reign of Charles II. and James II. transportation was extensively employed.

Transportation in those days was, in five cases out of six, a sentence which left the convict no hope of return, for those who survived the frightful hardships of the convict hulks, perished in great numbers under the rigours of the slavery which existed in the plantations of the West Indies and America. Hundreds of Quakers were transported during the reign of Charles II. While one ship, with 54 of them on board, lay in the Thames, 27 died. At least 800 of the farm labourers, weavers and colliers who had formed part of Monmouth's army were sold off to English bidders, and transported to the West Indies, following the Bloody Assize, in the reign of James II. After the achievement of American independence in 1776, most of the convicts were shipped to Australia, there to create difficulties which lasted for 80 years.

Until 1840 English Judges passed long and savage sentences of transportation for the most trivial offences. In 1827 a youth of 18 was sentenced to transportation for life for stealing a pocket handkerchief. As we have already seen at the Salisbury Spring Assizes, 1830, Mr. Justice Gazelee had 130 prisoners before him, and he passed sentence of death on 29; life transportation on five; 14 years transportation on five; and seven years on 11. The Justices at Quarter Sessions were as cruel. For stealing a plank ten feet long a farm labourer was sentenced at Salisbury Quarter Sessions to 14 years transportation, the owner, a great local magnate, sitting on the Bench.

"In 1830, the farm labourers, driven wild by grinding poverty, and the threat of unemployment owing to the introduction of machinery, rose, and there was some rioting. It was mercilessly put down, and Special Commissions sat at Salisbury, Winchester and other places. At Salisbury 34 poor fellows were sentenced to death; 33 to be transported for life, ten for 14 years, and so on. "From all over the Plain their womenfolk had come to learn their fate . . . The sentenced men came out, looking eagerly until they recognised their own people, and cried out to them to be of good cheer . . . 'Don't go on so, old mother, 'tis only for life I'm sent.' . . . And yet another 'Don't you cry, old girl, 'tis only 14 years I've got, and maybe I'll live to see you all again' . . . And so on, as they filed past their weeping women on their way to Fisherton Gaol, to be taken thence to the transports in Portsmouth and Plymouth harbours waiting to convey their living freights to the hell on earth so far from home ... Not criminals, but good brave men were these—Wiltshire-men of that strong enduring, patient class, who, not only as labourers on the land, but on many a hard-fought field in many parts of the world have shewn the stuff that was in them.

"But, alas! for the poor women who were left—for the old mother who could never hope to see her boy again, and for the wife and children who waited and hoped against hope through long toiling years ... " (W. H. Hudson in "A Shepherd's Life.")

Even the Judges who sat on the Riots Commissions felt the cruelty of it all. The Hampshire Riot Commission, which sat at Winchester, had 600 prisoners to try, and on one day alone, out of 23 prisoners tried, 16 were sentenced to death. Writing to a friend that evening, Baron Alderson, one of the Judges, said: "I am thoroughly sick of the whole business, and hate it. These people have no idea of the risks they run, and will lose their lives without knowing why. They have been gulled and goaded on by a set of artful and unprincipled scoundrels.

"I have been trying a case under the Riot Act, and acquitted the prisoner on the ground of the proclamation not having been correctly made out, by the leaving out of 'God Save the King.' The Act is so very severe a law that one requires a very minute observance of all its provisions. I wish the punishment of death could be dispensed with."

Up to 1834 it was an offence for a convict to return from transportation. The punishment was death, yet many, drawn back by the uncontrollable longing to see their homes and loved ones again, risked the fearful consequences. The moving story of the convict who returned to England after a sentence of transportation for life has been told by Charles Dickens in "Great Expectations."

The man had been a desperate and dangerous man, but abroad he had reformed and prospered. His gratitude to the boy who had befriended him, and his great desire to see him again, brought him back to face almost certain death.

Re-captured, but severely injured and dying, he was committed to take his trial as a returned convict.

"The trial was very short and very clear. Such things as could be said for him were said—how he had taken to industrious habits, and had thriven lawfully and respectably. But nothing could unsay the fact that he had returned and was there in the presence of the Judge and Jury. It was impossible to try him for this and do otherwise than find him guilty.

"At that time it was the custom to devote a concluding day to the passing of sentences, and to make a finishing effect with the sentence of death. But for the indelible picture that my remembrance now holds before me, I could scarcely believe that I saw two-and-thirty men and women put before the Judge to receive that sentence together.

"Foremost among the two-and-thirty was he; seated, that he might get breath enough to keep life in him . . . .

"Then, the Judge addressed them. Among the wretched creatures before him, whom he must single out for special address, was one who almost from his infancy had been an offender against the laws: who, after repeated imprisonments and punishments, had been at length sentenced to exile for a term of years, and who, under circumstances of great violence and daring had made his escape and had been resentenced to exile for life. That miserable man would seem for a time to have been convinced of his errors and to have lived a peaceable and honest life. But in a fatal moment . . . he had quitted his haven of rest and repentance, and had come back to the country where he was proscribed . . . .

"The appointed punishment for his return to the land that had cast him out being death, and his case being an aggravated one he must prepare himself to die.

"The sun was striking in at the great windows of the court, through the glittering drops of rain on the glass, and it made a broad shaft of light between the two-and-thirty and the Judge, linking both together, and perhaps reminding some amongst the audience, how both were passing on, with absolute equality, to the greater Judgment that knoweth all things, and cannot err. Rising for a moment, a distinct speck of face in this ray of light, the prisoner said 'My Lord, I have received my sentence of Death from the Almighty, but I bow to yours,' and sat down again."

In 1834, the sentence of death for illegally returning from transportation was altered to penal servitude for life. Even though the man had led an industrious and honest life in the colony to which he had been transported and had prospered there, as some did, the punishment was the same; Justices and Constables shewed no mercy to the man who returned after a life sentence, or before his term expired.

In London, sentences were just as harsh as in the counties. W. Eden Hooper in "Newgate and the Old Bailey" gives many instances of Old Bailey sentences.

He says: "I will instance the case of John Eyre, a man of position, who was found guilty in 1771 of purloining a few sheets of printed paper. He was transported. Little more than a hundred years ago (1818) Dr. Halloran, tutor to the Earl of Chesterfield, received a similar sentence for forging a postage-paid mark, worth 10d."

When the furniture and fittings of the old Sessions House in the Old Bailey were on sale just before the new Court was opened in 1907, Mr. Hooper secured some of the records of indictments and sentences, and of the shipments of convicts.

"Under the endorsement of 'Morley Transport'" (he says) "was a list of 100 convicts embarked on board that vessel for New South Wales, from the Dolphin Hulk at Chatham on July 29th, 1829. Set forth in tabular form were the names and descriptions of the poor creatures sent out to the horrors of the penal settlements, together with their crimes and sentences.

Here are a few taken at random. Stealing an apron, sent for life; bacon, life; worsted yarn, life; 2 lbs. of potatoes, 14 years; a pair of shoes, 14 years; a bottle of spirits, 14 years.

Most of the convicts were young men, and quite a number only boys. Here is another record (one of the many thousands which those old faded blue sheets

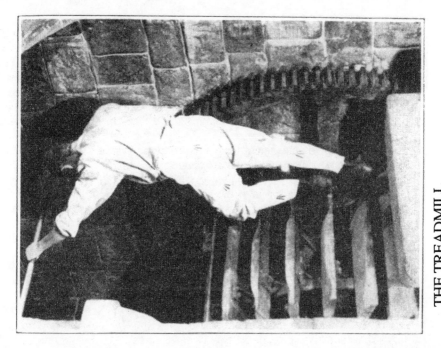

THE TREADMILL
(By courtesy of Mdme. Tussaud, Ltd.)

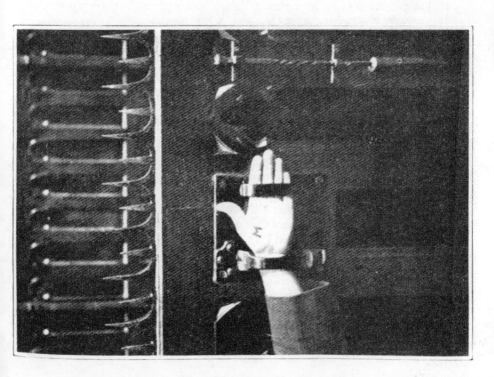

BRANDING IRON AT LANCASTER CASTLE

DONCASTER BODY IRONS

set forth) in the exact words: 'Charles Smith, age 17 years, attainted for felony. His Majesty having been graciously pleased to extend His Royal Mercy unto him upon condition of his being transported to the Coast of New South Wales or some one or other of the islands adjacent, for the term of his natural life, he was ordered by the Court to be transported accordingly. Dated this 27th day of July, 1829.'

And this was only a hundred years ago."

Even when the death sentence was commuted the convict could, if he or she preferred it, choose death.

Six women convicts in 1789 chose death rather than transportation. Five, on being brought back for sentence, after considerable hesitation, altered their minds and preferred exile to death. The sixth, Sarah Cowden, "a very young girl" convicted of robbery in a dwelling-house, peremptorily refused the alternative.

"The Recorder, in a very sensible and humane speech, admonished her of her danger. This unhappy and misguided girl, however, continued to refuse the proffered mercy. The Recorder was under the necessity of giving orders to the Sheriffs to prepare for her execution on Thursday morning.

"Whilst the unhappy wretch was taken from the bar to the cells, Mr. Garrow interposed in her favour, and begged that the Court would order her once more to the bar, to afford him an opportunity of shewing her the danger into which she had been precipitated by her obstinacy, and of endeavouring to persuade her to save her life, by accepting the King's mercy.

"The Court declared that her refusal was an affront to the humanity of the Sovereign, and that, unless she herself desired to return to the Court for the purpose of imploring forgiveness for her pertinacity her fate on Thursday morning was inevitable

"The idea of a poor, young and ignorant girl sacrificing her life to a mistaken principle of honour or to the more lamentable effects of bad advice, made an impression so deep and forcible, that Mr. Villette the ordinary, accompanied by Mr. Garrow and Mr. Leach, went into the prison, by the permission of the Court, and, after a quarter of an hour, returned with assurance that this misguided convict was sensible of her error, and desired to be brought to the Bar. She was accordingly conducted again into Court, and accepted life upon condition of exile.

"The Duchess of Cumberland and Mrs. Fitzherbert immediately withdrew, and the Court was adjourned." (Morning Chronicle, June 9th, 1789.)

If the following sentences from Mudies' "Felony of New South Wales" are to be believed some of the women convicts accepted their fate before they reached Australia and prepared to make the best of it:—

"When a female transport ship arrived at Sydney, all the madams on board occupy the few days which elapse before their landing in preparing to produce the most dazzling effect at their descent upon the Australian shore. Offers of marriage are made to some from the wayside, and at their new habitations they are besieged by suitors."

Whatever may have been the demeanour of the women on this particular convict ship, the fact is that, in the early days of transportation to Australia the outlook for the women, on arrival, was a terribly depressing one. Elizabeth Fry, who did a wonderful work for the poor women in Newgate and other prisons in the early nineteenth century, gives a description of their condition both on the ship and on landing. Her experience has been recorded by Elizabeth B. Emmott in "The Story of Quakerism."

"On arriving at the ship (the 'Maria') they found that below decks the prisoners were herded like cattle, some heavily ironed, and there they were to remain through all the weeks of the voyage, without any employment or oversight, and on their arrival at the penal settlement they would be turned out penniless and homeless in a strange land.

"It was quite evident that, unless something could be done for them, all the good they had gained in Newgate would be quickly undone. There was not much time to make arrangements, but Elizabeth Fry suggested that a monitor should be appointed over each mess of 12 women, and she exerted herself during the few days before they sailed in getting materials for knitting and patchwork to occupy them on the voyage, in the hope that, as there was a ready sale for these articles in the colony, the money they received might keep them from starving, until they could get some honest work.

"On the day that the 'Maria' sailed, Elizabeth Fry went on board, and, amid profound silence, read a few verses from the Bible, and prayed that God would bless these poor women, for whom she could do no more, and keep alive the good seed in their hearts . . . From this time until her death (1845) she visited every convict ship that left the Thames, except one."

CHAPTER XXV.

TREADMILL, THE CRANK, AND SHOT-DRILL

These appliances, installed in the prisons of the nineteenth century, while they were, at times, used for punishment of breaches of discipline in the prisons, were, primarily, part of the system of "hard labour" to which prisoners were committed. The treadwheel (or treadmill), shot-drill, the crank, the capstan, and stone-breaking, all formed parts of this system. There appears to have been some association between these useless and laborious forms of punishment and the introduction into the prisons of the cell system, the system of separate confinement. "The question arose, and was warmly debated, as to how hard labour could be adopted to the earlier system, and we find great ingenuity expended in devising forms of labour, such as cranks and treadwheels, in prisons in which each prisoner occupied a separate compartment." (Ruggles Brise in "The English Prison System.")

THE TREADMILL

The treadmill was a penal appliance introduced by Sir William Cubitt in 1818, and intended by him as a means for employing criminals usefully. It was a large hollow cylinder of wood on an iron frame, round the circumference of which were a series of steps about seven and a half inches apart.

The worker, steadying himself by a handrail above his head, trod on these, his weight causing the mill to commence to revolve, and compelling him to take each step in turn.

A very exact description of the working of the treadmill, and the effect upon the prisoners, is given in Henry Mayhew and John Binny's "Criminal Prisons of London" (1862). It is rather long but so well describes the punishment that the passage is given as it stands:—

"This invention was introduced at most of the prisons more than 40 years ago, but the machine, with but few exceptions, has never been applied, even to this day, to any useful purpose The prisoners style the occupation 'grinding the wind,' and that is really the only denomination applicable to it—the sole object of the labour of some 150 men, employed for eight hours a day, being simply to put in motion a big fan or regulator, as it is called which, impinging on the air as it revolves, serves to add to the severity of the work by increasing the resistance.

"Each wheel contains 24 steps, which are eight inches apart, so that the circumference of the cylinder is 16 feet. These wheels revolve twice in a minute, and the mechanism is arranged to ring a bell at the end of every thirtieth revolution, and so to announce that the appointed spell of work is finished. Every man put to labour at the wheel has to work for 15 quarters of an hour every day.

"Those who have never visited a correctional prison can have but a vague notion of a treadwheel. The one we first inspected at Coldbath Fields was erected on the roof of the large, cuddy-like room where the men take their meals. The entire length of the apparatus was divided into 24 compartments, each something less than two feet wide and separated from one another by high wooden partitions.

"When the prisoner has mounted to his place on the topmost step of the wheel, he has the same appearance as if he were standing on the upper side of a huge garden-roller, and somewhat resembles the acrobat we have seen at a circus perched on the cask that he causes to revolve under his feet.

"All the men work with their backs toward the warder supporting themselves by a hand-rail fixed to the boards at the back of each compartment, and they move their legs as if they were mounting a flight of stairs; but with this difference, that instead of their ascending, the steps pass from under them, and as one of the officers remarked, it is this peculiarity which causes the labour to be so tiring, owing to the want of a firm tread. The sight of the prisoners on the wheel suggested to us the idea of a number of squirrels working outside rather than inside the barrels of their cages.

"Only every other man out of the 24 composing the gang on the wheel, work at the same time, each alternate prisoner resting himself while the others labour. When we were at the prison, some of those off work, for the time being, were seated at the bottom of their compartment reading, with the book upon their knees; others, from their high place, were looking listlessly down upon some of their fellow-prisoners who were at exercise in the yard beneath, going through a kind of 'follow my leader' there. In the meantime, those labouring in the boxes on the wheel were lifting up their legs slowly as a horse in a ploughed field, while the thick iron shaft of the machinery, showing at the end of the yard, was revolving so leisurely, that we expected every moment to see it come to a standstill. We soon learnt that 'grinding the wind' was such hard labour that speed could not be given to the motion of the machine.

"Whilst we were looking on, the bell rang, marking the thirtieth revolution, and instantly the wheel was stopped and the hands were changed. Those whose turn it was to rest came down from the steps with their faces wet with perspiration and flushed with exercise; while the others shut up their books, and, pulling off their coats jumped up to their posts. There they stood until, at the word of command, all the men pressed down together, and the long barrel once more began to turn slowly round.

"Those who left the wheel sat down and, taking out their handkerchiefs, commenced wiping the perspiration from their necks and foreheads.

"We inquired if the work was very laborious, and received the following explanation. 'You see the men can get no firm tread from the steps always sinking away from under their feet, and that makes it very tiring. Again, the compartments are small, and the air becomes very hot, so that the heat at the end of the quarter of an hour renders it difficult to breathe!'

"The power that has to be continuously exercised in order that the prisoners may avoid sinking with the wheel is equal to that of ascending or lifting a man's own weight, or 140lbs.; and certainly the appearance of the men proved that a quarter of an hour at such work is sufficient to exhaust the strongest for the time being."

It was later that the treadwheel became the treadmill when it was utilised for grinding corn, pumping water and other prison purposes.

At Northallerton Gaol, the labour of the prisoners on the treadmill was formerly let out, on contract, to the local miller, who fixed the amount of power he wanted each day, and gave the prisoners a hard day or an easy one according to his own needs.

An unconvicted inmate of Northallerton Gaol, faced with the uncongenial alternatives of a bread-and-water diet or the treadmill, applied to the High Court for a mandamus to compel the Justices to afford him better treatment.

The Court held that the Justices had full discretion as to the kind of work to be imposed, and that even untried prisoners could not insist on being maintained in idleness!

Female prisoners were put to the treadmill in some prisons. At Brixton the treadmill cost over £7,000 to build. The treadmill at Holloway House of Correction had 24 compartments, the eight smaller ones being for juveniles.

Here the labour was utilised to pump the water supply for the prison from a deep well to storage tanks on the top of the building. The average distance travelled by prisoners on the wheel at this prison was 6,500 feet in winter and about 8,700 feet in summer, a distance much below the average for the prisons in London.

Adjoining the treadmill at Holloway Prison was a shed fitted with 24 compartments each containing a pump-handle at which prisoners worked to supplement the treadmill as it pumped the water.

THE CRANK

By the Prison Act of 1865, a male prisoner over 16 sentenced to hard labour, had to spend three months at least of his sentence in labour of the first class. Frequently the treadmill was the appliance employed, but sometimes the crank was used. The latter consisted of a small hand-wheel, like the paddle-wheel of a steamer, revolving in a box. The resistance was determined in different ways—by sand or gravel in the box; by a brake, or by weights. At Wandsworth Prison the normal resistance, without weights, was 7 lbs., but two weights added to it increased the resistance to 10 lbs., and the whole of the weights allowed brought it to 12 lbs. There were a hundred such machines at this prison. The average number of revolutions to be made was 12,000, and it appears to have been an exhausting occupation. Sometimes, it is said, the dial was not accurate and registered too few revolutions, and it appears to have been admitted that it was difficult to keep it accurate.

Messrs. Mayhew and Binny's description of the crank is, like that of the treadmill, so authoritative that it is quoted in full:—

"Sometimes a prisoner, tired of working at the tread-wheel, or fatigued with the monotony of working at his trade as a tailor, or cobbler, will complain of some ailment, such as pains in the back or chest, thereby hoping to obtain a change of labour. In such instances the man is sent to the surgeon to be examined. If he be really ill he is ordered rest; but if, as often, he is 'merely shamming,' then he is sent back to his former occupation. Should he still continue to complain he is set to crank-labour, and it is said that after a couple of days at this employment, the most stubborn usually ask to return to their previous occupation.

"Crank-labour consists in making 10,000 revolutions of a machine, resembling in appearance a 'Kent's Patent Knife-cleaner,' for it is a narrow iron drum, placed on legs, with a long handle on one side, which, on being turned, causes a series of cups or scoops in the interior to revolve. At the lower part of the interior of the machine is a thick layer of sand, which the cups, as they come round, scoop up and carry to the top of the wheel where they throw it out and empty themselves, after the principle of a dredging-machine. A dial-plate, fixed in front of the iron drum, shows how many revolutions the machine has made.

"It is usual to shut up in a cell the man sent to crank labour, so that the exercise is rendered doubly disagreeable by the solitude. Sometimes a man has been known to smash the glass in front of the dial-plate and alter the hands; but such cases are of rare occurrence.

"As may be easily conceived, this labour is very distressing and severe; but it is seldom used excepting as a punishment, or, rather, as a test of feigned sickness. A man can make, if he work with ordinary speed, about 20 revolutions a minute, and this, at 1,200 the hour, would make his task of 10,000 turns last eight hours and 20 minutes."

THE SHOT-DRILL

Turning again to Mayhew and Binny's great book for a description of the shot-drill, there is to be found an excellent picture of this exacting and useless form of punishment, to which there is no need to add one word (the prison referred to is the House of Correction at Coldbath Fields):—

"This most peculiar exercise takes place in the vacant ground at the back of the prison, where an open space, some 30 feet square and about as large as a racket court has been set apart for the purpose, on one side of the plantations of cabbages and peas. There is no object in this exercise beyond that of fatiguing the men and rendering their sojourn in the prison as unpleasant as possible.

"We took up one of these balls to examine it, and were surprised at its weight; for although not larger than a cocoanut, it required a considerable effort to lift it.

"The shot-drill takes place every day at a quarter-past three and continues until half-past four. All prisoners sentenced to hard labour, and not specially

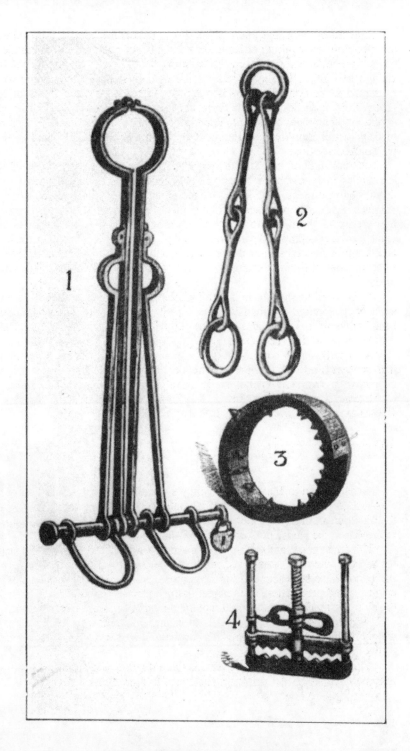

CELL WITH PRISONER AT "CRANK LABOUR" IN THE
SURREY HOUSE OF CORRECTION

excused by the surgeon, attend it; those in the prison who are exempted by the medical officer wear a yellow mark on the sleeve of their coat. Prisoners above 45 years of age are generally excused, for the exercise is of the severest nature and none but the strongest can endure it. The number of prisoners drilled at one time is 57, and they generally consist of the young and hale.

"The men are ranged so as to form three sides of a square, and they stand three deep, each prisoner being three yards distant from his fellow. This equidistance gives them the appearance of chess-men set out on a board. All the faces are turned towards the warder, who occupies a stand in the centre of the open side of the square. The exercise consists in passing the shot, composing the pyramids at one end of the line, down the entire length of the ranks, one after another, until they have all been handed along the file of men, and piled up into similar pyramids at the other end of the line; and when that is done the operation is reversed and the cannon balls passed back again. But what constitutes the chief labour of the drill is, that every prisoner at the word of command has to bend down and carefully deposit the heavy shot in a particular place, and then on another signal to stoop a second time and raise it up. It is impossible to imagine anything more ingeniously useless than this form of hard labour.

"A warder near to us, with whom we conversed, said 'It tries them worse taking up, because there's nothing to lay hold of, and the hands get hot and slippery with the perspiration, so that the ball is greasy like. The work makes the shoulders very stiff too.'

"This exercise continues for an hour and a quarter. We counted the distance that each man walked over in the course of a minute, and found that he traversed the three yards' space 14 times. According to this, he would have to walk altogether about one mile and three-quarters, picking up and putting down, at every alternate three yards, a weight of 24 lbs. It is not difficult to understand how exhausting and depressing such useless work must be."

In 1895, there were 39 treadmills and 29 cranks in use in English prisons, but these had dwindled down to 13 and five respectively by 1901, and both have been abolished for some years.

The system of hard labour seems to have varied greatly in the prisons, for when the prisons were taken over by virtue of the Act of 1877, it was found that at some prisons, such as Winchester, the whole prison population were employed in pumping, grinding and oakum-picking. At Oxford, the tread-mill, shot-drill, and capstan were usually employed. At Devizes, 62 out of 78 prisoners were engaged on the treadmill or in oakum-picking. Of the London prisons, Wandsworth specialised in the crank, and did not favour the treadmill, while at Coldbaths Prison, treadmill, crank, shot-drill and oakum-picking were all used by the prison authority.

The attempts made in the eighteenth century to provide prisoners with adequate employment in confinement failed owing to their uselessness. Both the treadmill and the crank were eventually made, to a certain extent, to serve useful purposes, but the whole system underwent drastic revision towards the end of the century, and there have been constant changes of policy in the present century, which cannot be entered into here.

CHAPTER XXVI.

OAKUM-PICKING

One of the chief difficulties experienced in prison administration for over a century has been that of finding suitable employment for prisoners sentenced to hard labour. The growth of trade unionism has added to this difficulty.

For many generations the prisons relied upon the oakum trade as a means of employment for prisoners, but this trade collapsed rather suddenly, about the middle of the last century owing to the substitution of iron and steel for wood in the building of ships, and as the steel ship has more and more supplanted the wooden ship, the prison authorities have had considerable difficulty in finding alternative employments.

Oakum is obtained by shredding, that is picking, "Junk," which is the name for old ship's cables and other ropes, made from tarred hemp. In the days of the wooden ships it was used in vast quantities, with pitch, for caulking the seams in the sides and decks of ships, and as the tasks imposed in the prison required the picking of a considerable quantity of this material by each prisoner it was a trying and monotonous occupation, very trying to the fingers.

A small quantity is still picked in the prisons to-day for use in small sailing ships and barges, but other occupations have largely taken the place of oakum-picking in the prisons.

Some writers appear to think that oakum, and "coir," (another substance used to provide prison labour) were one and the same thing, but this is not so, coir being the fibre of the cocoanut. It is still used for the making of mats, mattresses and pillows in prison. It is supplied to the prisons in two forms (a) coir fibre and (b) coir yarn. The fibre is purchased and used to fill prison mattresses, and, to some extent, to make special mats supplied to other Government departments. The yarn is purchased for the manufacture of door mats, gymnasium mats, matting, etc.: for the use of other state departments, different grades of fibre being used for the different purposes for which they are required.

In the present day the yarn is purchased ready-made, and the fibre is not twisted into yarn by prison labour, as in former days. The picking of coir is now limited to the re-picking of coir fibre removed from prison mattresses.

At Cold Baths Prisons, the former Middlesex house of correction for adult males, oakum-picking was performed in a room accommodating 500 men, and in dead silence. "If a man rested a moment he was encouraged and cheered to further industry by seeing on the walls the improving texts 'It is good for a man that he bear the yoke in his youth'; 'Godliness with contentment is a great gain'; 'Go to the ant, thou sluggard, consider her ways to the wise.'

"The discipline was such that, in 1854, out of the prison population of 9,180 no less than 9,023 were punished for making noises, insolence, and bad language!" (Albert Crew in "London Prisons.")

The description of the oakum-picking at this prison, by Henry Mayhew and John Binny, in "Criminal Prisons of London" (1862) gives a striking impression of the scene in the great oakum-picking shed:

"On the side fitted with windows the dark forms of the warders are seen, each perched up on a raised stool. The bright light shines on the faces of the criminals, and the officer keeps his eye rapidly moving in all directions, to see that no talking takes place . . . The utter absence of noise struck us as absolutely terrible. The silence seems after a time, almost intense enough to hear a flake of snow fall . . . .

"Each picker has by his side his weighed quantity of old rope, cut into lengths. Some of the pieces are white and sodden-looking as a washer-woman's hands, whilst others are hard and black with the tar upon them. The prisoner takes up a length of junk, and untwists it, and when he has separated it into so many corkscrew strands he further unrolls them by sliding them backwards and forwards on his knee with the palm of his hand, until the meshes are loosened

"Then the strand is further unravelled by placing it in the bend of a hook, fastened to the knees, and sawing it smartly to and fro, which soon removes the tar and grates the fibres apart. In this condition, all that remains to be done is to loosen the hemp by pulling it out like cotton wool, when the process is completed.

"By the rays of sunlight shining through the window you can see that the place is full of dust; the shoulders of the men, too, are covered with the brown dust almost as thickly as the shirt-front of a snuff-taker. A prisoner with a bright water-can is going the round, handing up drink to the warders, who gulp it down as if choked.

"As the day advanced, the pieces of old rope by the prisoners' sides disappeared bit by bit, and in their place the mound of treacle-brown oakum at their feet grew from the size of a scratch-wig to that of a large pumpkin. At length the men had all completed their tasks, and each sat holding on his knees his immense tar-covered ball, waiting to take his turn to go to the scales and have his pickings weighed.

"Then the silence of the room, which has all along been like that of a sick-chamber, is suddenly broken by the warder calling out 'The first three men!' Three grey forms rise up obediently as shepherd's dogs, and carrying their bundles before them, advance to the weighing-machine.

"We enquired if oakum-picking was a laborious task. 'Not to the old hands,' was the answer, 'We've men here that will have done their three or four pounds a couple of hours before some of the fresh prisoners will have done a pound. They learn the knack of it, and make haste to finish, so as to be able to read, but to the new arrivals it's hard work enough for most thieves' hands are soft, and the hard rope cuts and blisters their fingers, so that until the skin hardens it is very painful"

At Tothill Fields Prison, the other Middlesex House of Correction, *reserved for boys under 17*, and women (there was room for 300 boys) oakum-picking was the chief work, each prisoner picking from 1 lb. to 2 lb. daily. It was estimated that each boy prisoner cost £8, and that he earned about 17s. in one year by his labour. Over 6,000 women passed through this prison in a year, and the records of the prison shew that 40 to 50 per cent were always on the sick list. Their chief occupation was also oakum-picking, carried out in strict silence. Here, in the winter, the women were locked up at 6 p.m. in the dark and the cold, to pass the next 12 hours.

THE RACK

PUNISHMENT STOCKS AT KNARESBOROUGH

CHAPTER XXVII.

MISCELLANEOUS PUNISHMENTS

(1) BOILING TO DEATH

There are few instances of boiling to death as a punishment until the year 1531 when, and for a few years following, it became the law that prisoners should be so executed.

How far Henry the Eighth, a man of many crimes, was personally responsible for the horrible law passed in his reign which legalised this dreadful method of putting to death, will always be uncertain, but he was so infamously cruel that it is quite within the bounds of probability that he could be held responsible.

The preamble of the Act of 1530-1 was as follows:—

"On the Eighteenth day of February, 1531, one Richard Roose, of Rochester, Cook, also called Richard Cooke, did cast poison into a vessel, full of yeast or baum, standing in the kitchen of the Bishop of Rochester's Palace, at Lambeth March, by means of which two persons who happened to eat of the pottage made with such yeast died," and the Act went on to enact that: "The said poisoning be adjudged high treason; and that the said Richard Roose, for the said murder and poisoning of the said two persons, shall stand, and be attainted of high treason, and shall be therefore boiled to death, without benefit of clergy. And that, in future, murder by poisoning shall be adjudged high treason, and the offender deprived of his clergy and boiled to death."

The grounds for this extraordinary definition of high treason were not given, but, as the pot of food, it is stated elsewhere, was intended for the consumption of poor persons of the neighbourhood, it is somewhat difficult to understand how the crime could have affected the King or the State.

Roose was taken to Smithfield, and killed in this most barbarous way on the 15th of April, 1532, but as a young woman, a maid servant, had been executed by boiling to death a little before this date (in 1531), there seems to be some doubt as to whether the new statute was merely a re-enactment of a previous Act, or whether it gave legal countenance to a practice which had been in use from some earlier date. The earlier execution took place in the Market Place at King's Lynn.

There is one other case on record of this peculiarly cruel method of putting to death, and in this case the woman Margaret Davy, also a maid-servant, who had poisoned the persons with whom she lived, perished at Smithfield in March, 1542.

William Andrews (in "Bygone Punishments") says that the punishment had been common, both in England and on the Continent, before the passing of Henry's Act, as a punishment for coining. He quotes a case, referred to in the "Chronicles of the Gray Friars of London," in which a man was fastened to a chain, at Smithfield, and let down into boiling water several times until he was dead.

This fearful punishment did not long disgrace the statute-book, for immediately following the death of Henry the Eighth, it was repealed in the first year of the reign of his son Edward the Sixth, in 1547, and, thenceforward, poisoning again came under the heading of murder, without benefit of clergy.

(2) ENGLISHRY

Englishry, or presentation of Englishry, was a simple device of the Normans for the protection of their own people in a foreign and hostile country, such as England was in the early years of the Conquest.

There is some evidence that the idea was not an original one, but that it was used by Canute, for the protection of his Danes, but in Norman times it became a well-established principle

The Norman lords oppressed the English peasantry, and the peasantry took their revenge by murdering their retainers, or even the lords themselves, if opportunity occurred. As the peasants stood loyally by each other, it was exceedingly difficult to discover the perpetrators of these crimes. It was ordained, therefore, that when a man was found dead, and there was evidence that he had been murdered, and the slayer could not be identified, the hundred in which the murder had been committed would be heavily fined.

The fine imposed was known as a "murdrum." In many assizes of the thirteenth century numerous "murdra" were exacted from the unfortunate English inhabitants of the hundreds.

It was assumed that the dead man was a Norman, but if the men of the hundred could prove that he was an Englishman they escaped penalty, but proof that the dead man was an Englishman could be given only by his kinsfolk.

It is probable that, as the English and Norman peoples merged into one race, this law was less and less seriously enforced, but it remained, in fact, the law of the land until the reign of Edward III., when, by the Act of 1340 A.D. it was enacted that "because many mischiefs have happened in divers counties of England, which had no knowledge of presentment of Englescherie, whereby the Commons of the Counties were often amerced before the Justices in Eyre (the Judges of Assize), to the great mischief of the people, it is assented that, from henceforth, no Justice in Eyre shall put in any Article of Opposition. Presentment of Englescherie against the Commons of the Counties, nor against any of them, but that Englescherie and Presentment of the same be wholly ousted for ever, so that no person by this cause may be from henceforth impeached."

What were the "many mischiefs" suffered by the Counties which led to this repeal of the old law is not known. It would seem that the original purpose of the "murdrum" or fine had been perverted from its original use, and that the Judges were using it as a source of revenue for the King, as a large proportion of the fine went to the Crown, a small amount being allotted to the relatives of the murdered man.

(3) FINES FOR MINOR OFFENCES

While there is abundance of material as to the punishments inflicted by the sentences of Courts of Assize and Quarter Sessions, there is very little information available as to the methods by which the Justices dealt with minor offences brought before the local Courts. The following list of fines, extracted by Mr. J. R. Witty from the Beverley Town Records is, therefore, of considerable interest, and throws some light upon the breaches of the law brought before the Justices of a typical country market town. In the case of Beverley, it has to be borne in mind that the power of the Archbishop of York extended even to the appointment of the Justices, and that he received all fines imposed by the local Court. There is an indenture of November 5th, 1536, made between the Archbishop and the burgesses of the town, which sets out the agreement to that effect:—

"He retains his own Court Leet, and the perquisites thereof. He is the authority to appoint the Clerk to the Markets" (presumably receiving the tolls collected from the market) "and retains the sole right to make justices of the peace having the same powers within the town as those by the King elsewhere, but he receives all fines from defaulters inflicted by these same Justices."

Human nature, it will be seen was very much as it is to-day; there is the profiteer, who sells shoes of inferior quality, or overcharges for candles; the butcher selling doubtful meat; the men who, defiant of the primitive public health regulations, leave the gutters choked up with refuse, or leave a dead pig in the street; who abuse those in authority, and so on.

The Alderman who brought the town into contempt by his poor play at the Pageant, was not only held up to contempt for his poor dramatic work, but was smartly fined!

1558 Fines of 4d. each for having pigs in the Churchyard; 4d. for a pig straying into the common street.

1557 Robt. Farrer, 16d. for saying words in abuse of his brethren the Governors.

1545 Fine of 2d. for leaving wood in the street.

1520 Richard Trollop, Alderman of Painters, fined 2/- because his Play, of The Three Kings (in the Pageant plays) was badly played in contempt of the community, when strangers were present.

John Peake, 8d. for selling a measly pig in the common market.

1502 Wm. Hewson, cooper, fined 12d. for speaking malicious words in the town and in taverns saying that Charters belonging to the town and community were either absent or stolen.

1494 John Belton, weaver, fined 2d. for abusing the common Sergeant while in the execution of his offfice. Robt. Smith, walker, for refusing to bury a dead pig, 8d.

1576-7 Feb. 21st. J. Robinson, fined 3/4 for brewing unlicensed.

1577 June 25th. Thos. Green fined 1/- for not paying to the poor.

1576 Nov. 29th. Jn. Reade, for having uncleansed gutters, 3d.

1576-7 Feb. 7th. Jas. Hartas, otemeall maker, for drying oats upon the Saboth day, 3/4.

1577 July 11th. Jno. Parkinson, Boocher, for killing a bull unbaited against th'order, 2/-.

1577 Aug. 8th. Wm. Lowson, butcher, for selling flesh in the market not marketable, 6d.

1577 Aug. 15th. Jno. Levytt, for making paire of shoes of unlawfull stuffe, 4d.

1577 Sept. 12th. Several items of 4d. each for "dogges unmussled."

1578 April 24th. Bart. Somme, 5/- for selling wares before the Fayre was opened.

1578 Oct. 30th. Four fined 3/4 each for selling candles above the price assigned them by the Mayor (profiteering).

(4) FORFEITURES

In former days convictions for the more serious offences, such as treason, misprision (concealment) of treason, felony, murder, praemunire, and striking or threatening a judge, led to partial or complete forfeiture of the offender's property, and, in many cases, the convicted criminal, in addition to any other penalty which he suffered, was left penniless.

Sometimes the forfeiture comprised the lands and tenements; in other cases the profits of the lands were forfeited. In treason the forfeiture began from the day of the treason, so as to nullify all intermediate sales or transfers.

With one exception, all these forfeitures came to an end by the passing of the Forfeiture Act, 1870, which enacted that all forfeitures of lands and goods for treason or felony were abolished. Misprision of treason is an indictable misdemeanour and, doubtless by an oversight, the forfeiture in this case was not abolished, as the Act relates only to treasons and felonies, so that a person convicted of concealment of treason might still be deprived of the profits of his lands for life.

The principle of forfeiture still exists in a number of cases. Motor-car licences, pawnbrokers' licences, and moneylenders' licences may still be forfeited for certain specified offences: gunpowder may be forfeited if an Inspector under the Explosives Acts is obstructed on searching premises; guns and nets of poachers searched on the highway, and found upon them, may be confiscated upon conviction; and certain pensions may be taken away from pensioners sentenced to imprisonment with hard labour, or to penal servitude.

Salmon-poachers may still be ordered to lose fish and fishing tackle, and there is power to order the forfeiture of many other articles—pirated music, cigarettes, intoxicating liquor, betting-books, game, firearms and ammunition—under various Acts of Parliament.

(5) PENANCE

Ecclesiastical punishments were generally more merciful than those inflicted under the criminal law of the State, though with regard to witchcraft and heresy, the two deadly sins, the Church shewed no mercy.

The clergy were forbidden by their own laws to inflict either death or mutilation. In Anglo-Saxon days the bishop sat in the county court, but later the ecclesiastical judges were withdrawn from the secular courts, and thenceforward for centuries, they sat in their own courts. It is impossible to deal with the history of these courts, or to go into the long dispute between State and Church as to the extent of their jurisdiction. It is sufficient to remember that the Church finally acquired jurisdiction over all "clerks," a vast body of persons who could not be punished in the State criminal courts, and, as a result, it dealt with a multitude of criminal acts, committed by its adherents. It could punish by life-long imprisonment, and by fines, but being debarred from the punishments of death and mutilation, methods freely employed by the State courts, it evolved a system of penitential discipline.

It could refuse access to Church or Communion, and thereby (as was firmly believed in mediaeval days) thrust the criminal into the outer darkness, a terrible punishment to the superstitious and the ignorant. The Bishop could degrade the clerk from his orders, and as an additional punishment relegate him to a monastery, or keep him in prison for life. He could order whipping, and Thomas a Beckett, it would appear, had recourse to the branding iron, but broadly, the system of punishment was built up on penances of many kinds. The wrong-doer might be ordered to undertake a pilgrimage; to abstain from certain foods, or, alternatively, to exist for a specified time (sometimes for years) on bread and water. Our own King Edgar was condemned not to wear his crown for seven years. Henry II. was ordered to undertake a pilgrimage of penitence to the tomb of Becket. He was severely scourged by 80 ecclesiastics, the bishops giving five strokes each, and every monk three. The King's penance brought on illness.

But the authority of the Church was final, and there were, undoubtedly, methods by which penances could be mitigated. The rich could perform their pilgrimages vicariously, that is to say, by deputy, and there arose a class of professional pilgrims, ready to undertake any task upon suitable recompense. A rich man condemned to fast could take other men to share his fast. If the fast were for 39 days, with 12 assistants, the penitent could perform his penance in three days, living on bread, raw
herbs and water.

Later we find magistrates, as well as clergy, ordering those, for instance, who had been guilty of insolence or insubordination to them, to do penance at Church, the offender being taken, at the close of service, to the local stocks for further punishment. There are numerous instances of women who had been guilty of immorality or unchastity being ordered to do penance in church. Many church registers contain records of such penances, and old churchwarden's accounts record purchases, or the hire, of black or white sheets for the penitent to wear on these occasions. On August 25th, 1850, a penance was performed in Wakefield Parish Church, by sentence of the Ecclesiastical Court, by a man who had defamed the character of a lady. A recantation was repeated by the penitent, after the Vicar, and then signed by the interested parties.

So recently as July 30th, 1882, a man performed a public penance in East Clevedon Church, Somersetshire.

(6) THE PICKET AND THE WHIRLIGIG

THE PICKET

The picket was a punishment of the army penal code, and appears to have been limited, for some reason, to the cavalry and artillery.

A post being driven into the ground, and a stool placed alongside it, the culprit was made to mount on to the stool, and, a noose being placed around one wrist, he was then hauled up so that he could barely touch the stool with his foot. A stump, rather higher than the stool, the top fashioned to a rough point, was driven into the ground alongside the post. The stool being removed, the naked heel of the criminal was placed on the point of the stump which, although it did not break the skin, caused, in a very short time, a most intolerable pain. The only relief to the prisoner was to swing by the wrist which caused a pain just as intolerable.

The length of time allotted to this punishment, although it was sometimes extended, was 15 minutes. The serious physical consequences which sometimes followed eventually led to the abolishment of this barbarous punishment.

It was largely used in Ireland, during the rebellion of 1798, upon those insurgents who had the misfortune to fall into English hands.

(The Doncaster historian, Hatfield, gives the above account of this unusual punishment, and it has been found impossible to verify his account. He also quotes a Captain Grose for the statement that only one form of corporal punishment could be inflicted upon an officer—this was boring the tongue with a hot iron for blasphemy—and that this remained in force during the reign of Queen Anne.)

THE WHIRLIGIG

The writer mentioned above, C. W. Hatfield, of Doncaster, is also the authority for the assertion that, formerly (no period is given), trifling offences were punished by the whirligig, a round wooden cage, turning on a pivot. The culprit was confined in this and whirled round with such velocity that extreme sickness ensued, a punishment highly distressing and dangerous. Whether this really happened—whether the whirligig was a local punishment—or whether Hatfield dreamed of it after an evening on a roundabout at Doncaster Fair, cannot now be decided!

(7) RIDING THE STANG

The ancient custom of holding up to ridicule, and to public condemnation, a man who had beaten his wife, or had been unfaithful to her, by what was called "Riding the Stang" was quite common in all parts of England until nearly the end of the nineteenth century. In contrast to such former punishments as the pillory or the stocks, in which the public could, and did, share by actual violence to the offender, this public exhibition of animosity towards him left him unharmed physically, unless the crowd could get hold of him, in which case he probably realised more fully that he was not a popular figure.

The method of carrying out the "punishment" was more or less the same everywhere. A long pole or ladder was used, on which was mounted an effigy of the offender, bearing a card round the neck setting out his offence. A "band"—of the tin-kettle variety—was formed, and buckets were used for drums The wittiest man in the crowd was selected to do the speech-making, and he recited a "nominy," or doggerel verse, of which there are several variants, but, roughly, it ran on the lines of the following:—

"Here we cum wiv a ran-a-dan-dan
It's neither for ma cause nor they cause that I ride this stang
But fir Bill . . . the shepherd, whose wife he did bang
E brayed her, he brayed her, he brayed her indeed,
E banged her poor creattur, afoor she stood need.
E took neeather belt, whip, iron nor stower,
Bud he up wiv a rowlin pin and knocked her ower.
Upstairs aback o bed
Sike a riot as nivver was led
Doon stairs aback o deear (door)
E bang'd her while her back was seear (sore)
Fooaks next dear heeard sike a jabber
Cos their tongues were liggin on hard as they could labber.
Poor thing was so scared at she ran iv a fullock
Then with coalrake a knockt her doon like a bullock.
She opponed her gob and she let oot a yowp
An he clooted her while she were stiff as a stowp.
Twas a sin and a shaame was's way that he tanned her
An HE mun leeak oot, else HE'll ger a back-ander
Noo all thoo good fowk wha live i this Raw (Row)
We'll hae thee tak notice for this is oor law
If onny o you husban's your gudwives you do bang
Let em cumtiv us, and we'll ride THOO a stang."

The spokesman mounted the "stang" with the effigy and both were carried round the village by the crowd, stops being made from time to time for the recital of the nominy. This was carried on for three nights, and each night the church was encircled by the procession, apparently under the belief that, as the proceedings went on for three nights, and the church was included in the route, there would be no subsequent proceedings for a breach of the peace!

On the third night the effigy was burnt, and the proceedings ended, doubtless to the satisfaction of the crowd, and to the great relief of the culprit.

A variation of this performance in the south of England was called "skimmington-riding," a cart or donkey being used for the conveyance of two persons, one representing the husband and the other the wife, who beat each other, the one with a skimmer, and the other with a ladle. The words "skimmington-riding" were derived from the skimming-ladle used in the ceremony. In Scotland, as in the north of England, the performance was called "riding the stang," but in Wales it was known as "riding the wooden horse."

The custom was a more or less harmless one, but it had the effect of intimidating the immoral husband or the wife-beater.

Mr. J. R. Witty, of Beverley, quotes the "nominy" given above, as one told to him by his mother. She had heard it in her young days from her grandmother, who witnessed several "stangings" about 1820.

BIBLIOGRAPHY

Many works have been consulted during the preparation of this book; those which have been of the greatest assistance to the author include the following:—

1. *THE ENCYCLOPAEDIA BRITANNICA* (14th Edition).
   Contains excellent articles upon many of the subjects of the foregoing Chapters.

2. *CRIMINAL PRISONS OF LONDON.* Henry Mayhew and John Binny, 1862 (Griffith Bone & Co.).
   A remarkable account of the London Prisons of 77 years ago. There is no book which gives so exhaustive and clear an account of the prison life of the period.

3. *LONDON PRISONS OF TO-DAY AND YESTERDAY*, 1933. Albert Crew (Ivor Nicholson & Watson, Ltd.).
   A concise and very readable book.

4. *HISTORY OF NEWGATE AND THE OLD BAILEY*, 1935. W. Eden Hooper (The Underwood Press, Ltd.)
   Now, unfortunately, out of print, but a sincere and scholarly account of London Prison life in former days.

5. *JUSTICE AND POLICE IN ENGLAND*, 1929. Albert Lieck (Butterworth & Co., Ltd.).
   A most valuable study, in the charming vein which distinguishes all Mr. Lieck's delightful volumes.

6. *A HISTORY OF PENAL METHODS*, 1914. George Ives (Stanley Paul & Co.).

7. *BYGONE PUNISHMENTS*, 1931. William Andrews (Philip Allan & Co., Ltd.).

8. *A HISTORY OF POLICE IN ENGLAND*, 1901. Captain W. L. Melville Lee (Methuen & Co.).
   A very able and practical history of the English Police.

9. *WAKEFIELD HOUSE OF CORRECTION*, 1904. J. Horsfall Turner (The Author).

10. *THE CONSTITUTIONAL HISTORY OF ENGLAND*, 1931. F. W. Maitland (Cambridge University Press).

11. *THE HISTORY OF ENGLISH LAW*, 1911. Pollock and Maitland (Cambridge University Press).

12. *THE STORY OF QUAKERISM*, 1911. Elizabeth B. Emmott (Headley Brothers).

13. *WHARTON'S LAW LEXICON*, 1859. J. J. S. Wharton (Stevens & Norton).

14. *THE ENGLISH PRISON SYSTEM*, 1921. Sir Evelyn Ruggles-Brise (MacMillan & Co., Ltd.).

15. *THE WEST RIDING SESSIONS RECORDS*, 1915. Edited by John Lister for the Yorkshire Archaeological Society.

The author acknowledges his indebtedness to all these interesting and very helpful books and to their authors.

INDEX